The exhibition and catalogue *The Discourse of Events* is derived from work by students of Bernard Tschumi, Unit Master 1973-1979 and Nigel Coates, Unit Master 1979 to date.

Exhibition organised by Nigel Coates and advised by Bernard Tschumi, through the office of the Chairman, Alvin Boyarsky, assisted by Micki Hawkes.

Catalogue designed by Nigel Coates and Martin Benson. Produced by the Communications Unit co-ordinated by Dennis Crompton. Production editor June McGowan. Production by Christine Wallace, Nicki Roberts, Simeon Halstead and Ben Van Verkel. Typography by Virginia Charlery.
Exhibition mounted by Amanda Innes. Photography by Alistair Dunn and Paul Barnett.

This catalogue coincides with the exhibition from 4 March to 1 April 1983.

Cover illustration: Christina Norton, *Giant Sized Baby Town's Fabric Factory*, 1982.

© ARCHITECTURAL ASSOCIATION 1983
Printed in London by Spin Offset Ltd.
ISBN 0 904503 24 0

The Discourse of Events

CONTENTS

THEMES 3
ARCHITECTURAL ASSOCIATION
LONDON

Foreword

The *Themes* exhibitions document students' work produced within the Diploma School of the Architectural Association (years 4 and 5) since the advent of the unit system a decade ago.

The Discourse of Events introduces researches into design initiated by Bernard Tschumi in 1973 and follows their evolution through to the present day under the tutorship of Nigel Coates, one of the original band of students during the unit's formative years.

Following on from Themes I: *Architecture and Continuity*, prepared by Dalibor Vesely and Mohsen Mostafavi and Themes II: *Spirit and Invention* (Peter Cook, Ron Herron and Christine Hawley), the present exhibition highlights some of the characteristics of the unit system as it has developed: namely, the wide-ranging preoccupations, differences in pedagogical technique, aspirations and sense of style available and interacting, however subliminally, at any given moment.

In fact, the early seventies at the AA have emerged as a watershed for a number of overlapping reasons. The perennial struggle for the survival of an independently financed professional school reached its apex with the announcement of closure in 1971, thus effectively causing a near-cessation of activity after a decade of feverish invention and experiment by staff and students alike, work avidly reported in the pages of *AD* magazine.

In this respect the exhibition *70 New Architects* arranged by Peter Cook, showing the work of the 1971 graduating class, summed up another dilemma. In spite of the wit and charm of much of the work shown, there were only faint echoes of the exuberance and invention of the mainstream sixties. Gone was the cutting edge honed by the Smithson's revisionist attitudes towards the CIAM mandate and their curious topologies: gone too were the expediencies and the myth of a technological utopia spawned by Cedric Price and Archigram, including the efforts to achieve an architecture of short-life building, flexibility, growth and change, cybernetic control, necessary life-support systems and the magic of Cape Canaveral. Instead, the pop scene was at its peak, the hairshirt, brown rice brigade was about to make its move (garbage housing/street farming) and a certain amount of thoughtful introspection and self-parody were the order of the day.

Nevertheless, as has been pointed out in several of the contributions to this catalogue, there existed a quiet confidence in the future. In retrospect, the triggering device was the release of the then fifth year tutors from their supporting role, by offering space and a platform to develop and offer individual studio courses freely advertised to the student body. The visible outpouring of creative and intellectual energy which resulted, produced series of conversations and issues provoking the works of the last ten years to which the first three *Themes* exhibitions bear witness.

The Discourse of Events is particularly interesting as it represents the evolution of the unit's outlook and work over the entire period. Bernard Tschumi and Nigel Coates refer to the ambience of the early days, as tutor and student. They offer personal insights into continental influences via the various intellectual strains brought together for seminars and lecture series, the example of current artists and critics and their reactions to other activity underway in the school at the time. The starting point for the work of the unit was the programme, particularly as seen from the point of view of the individuals involved. Inevitably, this led to spatial interpretations more closely allied to the space of literature, films and performance than to traditional architectural modes, a corresponding development of notational systems, *in situ* experiments, appropriate graphic systems, special sympathy for the actions and life of some of the shabby but vital urban institutions of the moment and, more recently, to brave attempts at a synthesis, at city-scale, based on the grim economic realities of our time.

It remains to thank Bernard Tschumi and Nigel Coates for their considerable effort over the years and for the spirited response of the students, including their retrospective comments, whose examples have enormously enriched the activities of the school as a whole.

Alvin Boyarsky

5

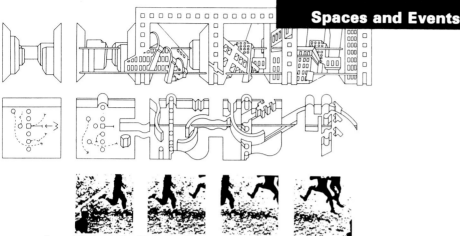

Bernard Tschumi, The Block, The Manhattan Transcripts, 1981

Bernard Tschumi

Publishing student projects makes sense only if the projects rise beyond the documentary quality generally offered by such publications and place themselves historically – either as a contribution to contemporary polemics or, in the best sense, as broader theoretical argument. The following work done by students in this unit at the Architectural Association over nearly ten years, first with myself, then with Nigel Coates, attempted just that: to make a contribution to general architectural discourse by stating that there is no space without event, no architecture without programme. It argued that the meaning of architecture – its social relevance and its formal invention – could not be dissociated from the events that 'happened' in it. It relentlessly insisted on issues of programme and representation. It stressed a critical attitude that observed, analysed and interpreted some of the most controversial positions of past and present architectural ideologies.

Yet the work often took place against the mainstream of the prevalent architectural discourse. For over the last decade, a specific phenomenon has occurred: the exacerbation of stylistic concerns at the expense of programmatic ones, the reduction of architecture as a form of knowledge to architecture as mere knowledge of form. From 'modernism' to 'postmodernism,' the history of architecture has surreptitiously been turned into a history of styles. This perverted form of history borrowed from semiotics the ability to 'read' layers of interpretation, but reduced architecture to a system of surface signs, at the expense of the reciprocal, indifferent or even conflictive relationship of spaces and events.

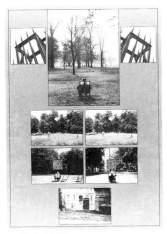

Nigel Coates, Prison Park, 1974

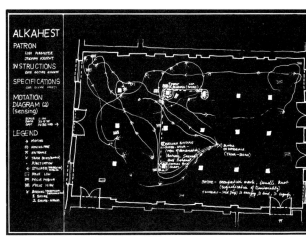

Derek Revington, Alkahest performance notation, 1975

This is not the place for an extensive analysis of a situation that has recently engulfed the critical establishment of architecture. However, it should be stressed that it is no accident that this emphasis on stylistic issues also corresponds to a double and wider phenomenon: on the one hand, to the increasing role of the developer in planning large buildings, encouraging many architects to become mere decorators of exteriors or interiors; and on the other, to the tendency of many architectural critics to concentrate on surface readings, signs, metaphors and other modes of presentation, often to the exclusion of spatial or programmatic concerns. These are two faces of a single coin, which typify the increasing desertion by the architectural profession of its responsibilities *vis-à-vis* the events and activities taking place in the spaces it designs.

But as I write today, the notion of programme is still forbidden territory. Programmatic concerns are rejected as leftovers from obsolete functionalist doctrines by those polemicists who see programmes as mere pretexts for stylistic experimentation. Few dare to explore the relation between the formal elaboration of spaces and the invention of programmes, between the abstraction of architectural thought and the representation of events. The popular dissemination of architectural images through eye-catching reproductions in journals and magazines often turns architecture into a passive 'object' of contemplation instead of the *place* that confronts spaces and actions. Most exhibitions of architecture in art galleries and museums encourage 'surface' practice and present the architect's work as a form of decorative painting. Walls and bodies, abstract planes and figures are rarely seen as part of a single and overall signifying system.

History, though, may one day look upon this period as the moment of the loss of innocence in 20th century architecture: the moment when it became clear that neither super-technology, expressionist functionalism nor neo-Corbusianism could solve society's ills, and that architecture was not ideologically neutral. A strong political upheaval, a rebirth of critical thought in architecture and new developments in history and theory in recent years all triggered a phenomenon whose consequences are still unmeasured. This general loss of innocence resulted in a variety of moves by architects according to their political or ideological leanings. In the early seventies, some denounced architecture altogether, arguing that its practice, in the current socio-economic context, could only be reactionary and reinforce the status quo. Others, influenced by structural linguistics, talked of 'constants' and the rational autonomy of an architecture which transcended all social forms. Others polemically reintroduced political discourse and advocated a return to pre-industrial forms of society (particularly Leon Krier, who was teaching at the AA at the time). And still others cynically took the analyses of style and ideology by Barthes, Eco or Baudrillard, and diverted them from their critical aims, turning them over like a glove: instead of using them to question the distorted, mediated nature of architectural practice, these architects 'injected' meaning into their buildings artificially, through a collage of historicist or metaphorical elements. The restricted notion

Ground hogs and carpets can both be mythical. It all depends on how you look at it. The groundhog comes out one day in late February after a long hibernation. If he sees his own shadow it is said that there will be at least six more weeks of winter. I've only seen one groundhog. I wanted to see if the weather would improve so I went out on the designated day and looked around. I was having difficulty when all of a sudden one appeared, sticking his head out above the ground. I realized that when he rose higher his head would be pointed away from the sun so that he would see his shadow. Being tired of winter and wanting better weather I shouted to distract him, hoping that he would turn my way and not see the shadow. Ironically, at the same time a woman came out of the house across the way and started shaking a carpet. I was surprised to see someone as lovely as she. He turned his head also, fascinated by the fluttering object. I tried to duck down so he wouldn't look back at me, thereby turning his head my way and perhaps catching a glance of the shadow. But as I lay there I couldn't see him anymore and had no way of knowing if he saw it or not. Thinking of this I got up, but he was gone. That March the weather was partly cloudy, sometimes snowing and sometimes sunny.

Bill Beckley, Ground Hogs and Carpets, 1975

of postmodernism that ensued – a notion diminished by comparison to those of literature or art – had completely and uncritically reinserted architecture into the cycle of consumption.

The unit's first programme was entitled *Theory, Language, Attitudes*. Using the AA structure, which encouraged autonomous research and independent lecture courses, it played on an opposition between certain political, theoretical and critical concerns about the city (those of Baudrillard, Lefèbvre, Adorno, Lukacs and Benjamin, for example) and an art sensibility informed by contemporary photography, conceptual art and performance. This opposition between a verbal critical discourse and a visual one suggested that they were complementary. Student projects explored that overlapping sensibility, often in a manner sufficiently obscure to generate initial hostility throughout the school. Most colleagues described our work as 'enigmatic' in front of us and 'mumbo-jumbo' behind our backs. Of course the codes used in the students' work differed sharply from the ones seen in schools and architectural offices at the time. Texts, tapes, films (the end-of-year exhibition space was filled with strips of 8mm film), manifestos, rows of story boards each with its own independent conventions, and photographs of ghost-like figures intruded an exhibition space arranged according to codes disparate from those of the architectural profession.

Photography was obsessively used: as 'live' insert, as artificial documentation, as a hint of reality interposed in architectural drawing – a reality nevertheless distanced and often manipulated, filled with skilful staging, with characters and sets in their complementary relations. Students used their persons to enact fictitious programmes inside carefully selected 'real' spaces, and then shot entire photographic sequences as evidence of their architectural endeavours. Any new attitude to architecture *had* to question its mode of representation. A project like Nigel Coates' *Prison Park* was as much about using a new code (insofar as photography is rarely used as a design tool) to describe a new content as about using a new content (the Prison Park) to discuss a particular code (photography) and its architectural implications.

Other works dealing with a critical analysis of urban life were generally written. They became a book edited, designed, printed and published by the unit; hence 'the words of architecture became the work of architecture,' as we said. Entitled *A Chronicle of Urban Politics*, the book attempted to analyse what distinguished our period from the preceding one, attempted to define the particular nature of the last quarter of the 20th century. Texts on fragmentation, cultural dequalification, and the 'intermediate city' analysed consumerism, totems, 'representationalism.' Some of the texts announced, several years in advance, preoccupations now common to the cultural sphere: dislocated imagery, artificiality, representational reality versus experienced reality.

This juxtaposition of verbal and visual led to the exhibition *A Space: A Thousand Words*, held at the Royal College of Art in early 1975. It gathered together thirty artists and architects ranging from Victor Burgin to John Stezaker, from Daniel Buren to Bill Beckley, from Christian de Portzemparc to Rem Koolhaas to Antoine Grumbach and

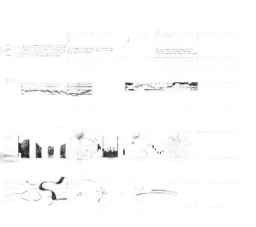

John Perver, The Opera and its Double, 1978

Murray John, Heartbreak Hotel, 1977

Peter Wilson, who all chose to oppose images and texts in a complementary manner. *A Space: A Thousand Words* was the first exhibition to bring artists and architects together around a common theme in an art context, a practice which has since been imitated as 'collaboration' (which is quite a different thing). This relationship between art and architectural discourse was reinforced by such events as the 'Real Space' conference, gathering Germano Celant, Bruce McLean, the group Nice Style, RoseLee Goldberg, Brian Eno, Rosetta Brooks, John Stezaker and other speakers and performers whose discourse or art practice we considered parallel to our own. My own lecture-performance with the musician Brian Eno was interrupted by sections of the audience shouting, 'Stop the music so we can *think*! Stop the talking so we can *listen*!'

The *mélange* of genres and disciplines was widely attacked by the academic establishment, still obsessed with concepts of disciplinary autonomy and self-referentiality. But the significance of such events is not a matter of historical precedence or provocation. In superimposing ideas and perceptions, words and spaces, these events underlined the importance of a certain kind of relationship between abstraction and narrative – a complex juxtaposition of abstract concepts and immediate experiences, contradictions, superimpositions of mutually exclusive sensibilities. This dialectic between the verbal and the visual culminated in 1974 in a series of 'literary' projects organised in the studio. Texts by Borges, Calvino, Hesse and Kafka provided programmes or events on which students were to develop architectural works.

The role of the text was fundamental in that it underlined some aspect of the complementing (or, occasionally, lack of complementing) of events and spaces. Some texts, like Calvino's metaphorical descriptions of 'Invisible Cities,' were so 'architectural' as to require going far beyond the mere illustration of the author's already powerful graphic description; Kafka's *Burrow* challenged conventional architectural perceptions and modes of representation, while Poe's *Masque of the Red Death* (done during my term as Visiting Critic at Princeton University) suggested parallels between narrative and spatial sequences.

Such explorations of the intricacies of language and space naturally had to touch on Joyce's significant discoveries. During one of my trips from the United States I gave extracts from *Finnegan's Wake* as the programme. The site was London's Covent Garden. The architecture was derived, by analogy or opposition, from Joyce's text. The complexities of Joyce and other writers obviously could not always be matched by their architectural projections, by visual parallels to their transpositions, derivations or oppositions. But the effect of such research was invaluable in providing a framework for the analysis of the relations between events and spaces, beyond usual functionalist or mechanistic notions.

The unfolding of events in a literary context inevitably suggested parallels to the unfolding of events in architecture. To what extent could the literary narrative provide light on the organisation of events in buildings, whether called 'use,' 'functions,' 'activities' or, ultimately, *'programmes'*? If writers could manipulate the structure of stories in the same way that they twist vocabulary and

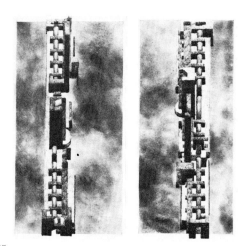

Chris Macdonald, New York Sequence, 1978

grammar, couldn't architects do the same, organising the 'programme' in a similarly objective, detached or imaginative way? For if architects could self-consciously use such devices as repetition, distortion or juxtaposition in the formal elaboration of walls, couldn't they do the same thing in terms of the activities that occurred within those very walls? Pole-vaulting in the chapel, bicycling in the laundromat, sky-diving in the elevator shaft. . .? Raising these questions proved increasingly stimulating: conventional organisations of spaces could be matched to the most surrealistically absurd sets of activities. Or vice-versa: the most intricate and perverse organisations of spaces could accommodate the everyday life of an average suburban family.

Such research was obviously not aimed at providing immediate 'answers,' whether ideological or practical. Far more important was the understanding that the relation between programme and building could be either highly sympathetic or, alternatively, contrived and artificial. The latter, of course, fascinated us more, as it rejected all functionalist leanings. It was a time when most architects were questioning, attacking or outright rejecting Modern Movement orthodoxy. We simply refused to enter these polemics, viewing them as stylistic or semantic battles. Moreover, if this orthodoxy was often attacked for its reduction to minimalist formal manipulations, we refused to enrich it with witty metaphors. Issues of intertextuality, multiple readings and dual codings had to integrate the notion of programme. After all, using a Palladian arch as an athletic club alters both Palladio and the nature of the athletic event.

As an exploration of the disjunction between expected form and expected use we began a series of projects opposing specific programmes with particular, often conflicting spaces. Programmatic context versus urban typology, urban typology versus spatial experience, spatial experience versus procedure and so on, provided a dialectical framework for research. We consciously suggested programmes that were impossible on the sites that were to house them: a Stadium in Soho, a Prison near Wardour Street, a Ballroom in a churchyard. At the same time, issues of *notation* became fundamental: if the reading of architecture were to include the events that took place in it, it was necessary to devise modes of notating such activities. Several modes of notation were invented to supplement the limitations of plans, sections or axonometrics. Movement notation derived from choreography and simultaneous scores derived from music notation were developed and elaborated for architectural purposes. (One student, Derek Revington, had already devised quite original modes of movement notation, coupled with live events, in his appropriation of a disused warehouse for an interpretation of Hesse's *Glass Bead Game.*)

If movement notation usually proceeded from our desire to map the actual movement of bodies in spaces, it increasingly became a sign that did not necessarily refer to these movements but rather to the *idea* of movement —a form of notation that was there to *recall* that architecture was also about the movement of bodies in space, that their language and the language of walls were ultimately complementary. Using movement notation as a

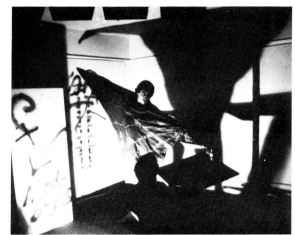

Drama, Situation, Scene, performance workshop, 1980

Carlos Villaneuva, Giant Sized Baby Town's Timber Fibre Factory, 1982

means of recalling issues was an attempt to include new and stereotypical codes in architectural drawing and, by extension, in its perception. This overlapping of images took a variety of forms, evident in Chris Macdonald or Murray John's layering of photographs, xeroxes and drawings. Such layerings, juxtaposition and superimposition of images purposefully blurred the conventional relationship between plan, graphic conventions and their meaning in the built realm. Increasingly the drawings became both the notation of a complex architectural reality *and* a drawing – an art work – in itself, with its own frame of reference, deliberately set apart from the conventions of architectural plans and sections.

The involvement of most students and faculty in the production of performances, videotapes and artists' books indicated a clear attempt to break apart the specific boundaries of the architectural discipline. The most recent work of the unit, as shown in the *Giant Sized Baby Town* project, is a case in point. Rather than using the specialist's mode of architectural representation (the axonometric, the plan, the section), it goes for the most popular form of architectural simulation: the perspective drawing, replete with atmospheric drama and narrative. But it differs in a fundamental manner from Serlio's, Le Corbusier's or SOM's perspectives. By using derivations of photographs or commercial or fashion designers' techniques; by overlaying them with artificially coded pastel pencil or brushstrokes, the work presents a sense of urgency missing from predecessors' work. This fascination for the dramatic, either in the programme (murder, sexuality, violence) or in the mode of representation

(strongly outlined images, distorted angles of vision – as if seen from a diving airforce bomber) is there to force a response. Architecture ceases to be a backdrop for actions, becoming the action itself.

All this suggests that 'shock' must be manufactured by the architect if his architecture is to communicate. Influence from the mass media, from fashion and popular magazines informs the choice of programmes: the lunatic asylum, the prison, the fashion institute, the Falklands War. It also influences the unit's graphic techniques, from the 'straight' black and white photography of the early days to the overcharged grease pencil illustration of recent years, stressing the inevitable 'mediatisation' of architectural activity. With the dramatic sense that pervades much of the work, cinematic devices replace conventional description. Architecture becomes the discourse of events as much as the discourse of spaces.

From the unit's early analytical days, when event, movement and spaces were carefully juxtaposed in their respective logic and mutual tension, the work has moved towards an increasingly synthetic attitude. We had begun with a critique of the city, had gone back to basics, to simple and pure spaces – to barren landscapes, a room; to simple body movements – walking in a straight line, dancing; to short scenarios. And we gradually increased the complexity by introducing literary parallels and sequences of events, placing these programmes within existing urban contexts. With the GSBT project, in which new programmes are placed in new urban situations, the process has gone full circle: it started by deconstructing the city, today it explores new codes of assemblage. ■

Nigel Coates, Muse Britannia, a museum of the Falklands war, 1982

Nigel Coates

Could it be that every version of the art avant-garde has at least one feature in common? Russolo gave concerts with industrial sirens, Duchamp upturned a urinal and called it a fountain, Joseph Beuys piled up fat in a corner – all of them used artefacts that were common enough but extraordinary to art. The greatest impact, it seems, can be caused by unsettling the things which are normally too ordinary even to be noticed.

The development of architectural ideas has usually depended on a different kind of operation – attacking the architecture of the time and replacing it with a new propagandist vision. At times when revolutionary ideas actually resulted in buildings, they at least had a symbiotic relationship with the rest of society. More frequently, however, architects have to make do with prediction, the old story of the architect with 'the mad ideas'. The fact that architecture need not 'progress' but can reappraise in the same manner as art has developed, has been swept up unnoticed in the not-so-progressive wind of modernism.

By the beginning of the seventies, however, an optimistic view of culture no longer adhered, certainly at least, not in terms of 'cities of tomorrow'. Yet it was through the work of Peter Cook and Archigram, that the AA had opened itself to a great deal of foreign, intellectual and political thought. Ironically, *Plug-in-City* had never been built, but the school in Bedford Square could at least try special, very unEnglish things within its enlightened academic boundaries. Circumstances were exactly right to form an art/experimental stream within the school.

The Discourse of Events traces the continuous arch-

Jenny Lowe, introduction to Five Spaces of a Day, 1975

Superstudio, Vita, from Five Stories, 1973

itectural endeavour of one so-called unit through the ten year period from its inception to its present role in the AA. Its work has always combined the art fringe with what is usually considered too ordinary to have anything to do with architecture. Yet within this, the unit has hardly stood still. Firstly, the focus has shifted from the sphere of the author towards architecture-in-use, and secondly, concerns and solutions have changed through the unit's particular sensitivity to the spirit of the time. Gradually, attitudes and working techniques have developed from the early conceptual preoccupations through to the current 'playground' drawings.

It was said from the beginning that architecture lay somewhere between the body and the city, that it was by no means exclusive, but *dependent* on the experiences it contained. It therefore had to consider fleeting meanings as well as solid architectural forms, movement as well as the volumes that contained them, the subjective as well as the rational – in fact, be an interpenetration of structures and life itself.

When Jenny Lowe and I joined the unit in 1973, our programmes were personal inventions specifically designed to orchestrate these oppositions. This resulted in using techniques not seen in the AA before – arranging photographs on a sheet so that they functioned like words or forming sequences of drawings that built up an increasingly abstract set of commentaries on architecture.

It was the time of architectural absolutes. Superstudio and Archizoom had produced elaborate parodies of 'the way architecture was going' with *No-Stop City* and *Five Stories* (Vita, Educazione, Cerimonia, Amore, Morte). Our own version of the absolute tended to subject architecture to our own demonstrative superimpositions. Buildings representing the inevitable political circumstances behind their production were defaced by personal gestures blown up to city-scale. We also frequently appeared in the works, 'clothed' in spatial structures – my body in a pyramid of cloth, or Jenny's wrapped up in gauze – so that architecture, or at least its essential marks, were connected to questions of existence.

The task was to clarify, to express architectural relationships through extremes. Design was restricted to refining the association of these images. . . a lot to do with symbols, archetypes, surrealistic interpretations of dreams. The aim was to investigate the total pattern of things, put it down on paper, and push the spectator to make what he could out of the pieces offered to him. In art, late conceptualism merged into performance; we were fascinated by the possible ironies that absolutes seemed capable of creating.

Involved in the continuous development of the unit, as I have been, it is easy to forget just how much the work has changed. As the material began to arrive for the show, a lot of the early works were shown to be far more straightforward than one remembers them, whether in terms of their content or the way they were executed. True, they had been done at a time before oil crises or terrorism had really taken hold. In 1974, some students in other units were still designing urban farms with solar panels on the roof and windmills in the garden. Long hair and platform shoes were what most people wore. It was *before* unemployment shot up, *before* video, *before* fast food,

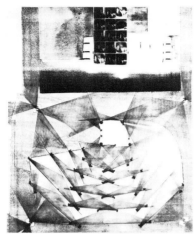

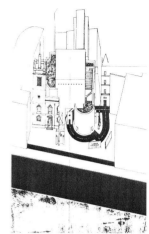

Jeremy Barnes, the Vatican Embassy, 1979

Socrates Panayides, St. Andrew's Exchange, 1980

walkmen or space-invaders. But the *attitude* of the unit was already established, if not the fully-fledged means of its expression.

In the following year, 1974-75, the briefs became more precise, and less operatic, alternating between projects like *A space for a friend* or those describing space as a mental paradox. These were intended to throw the question of design back on the author and then to use this subjective realism as a source for architectural form.

By the time of the *Joyce's Garden* project in 1977, there had been a hardening of the range of theoretical options on offer elsewhere in the school. Rationalism had developed the discussion of archetypes to a system of irreducible forms from which the events of the city would be entirely independent; other factions had returned to the nineteenth century or even earlier for inspirational models. Our work, however, now became more precise in a different manner. Programmes were set for hypothetically extreme types of building. The projects which resulted had a deliberately sombre classical atmosphere or what Chris Macdonald calls, 'the nuance more often consistent with reticence.

The language of classicism did influence activity in two important ways. Firstly, a building was not seen as the statement of a single idea... while the unit's study of space had shown meaning to depend on a kinetic continuum, the building could emphasise this by carefully orchestrating the elements it was made of, overstating certain parts and suppressing others, yet maintaining original forms sufficiently to underline the transformations they had undergone.

Secondly, the 'garden' was discussed as one kind of literary space which could be built, as the Renaissance and Baroque had shown. In the summer of 1976, Bernard Tschumi delivered a provocative, characteristically hyperbolic talk at Peter Cook's Art Net entitled, *The Garden of Don Juan*. In it he proposed that the lover's intrigue could be matched against the complexity of the garden; that desire could be architecture's substantive. In particular, gardens emphasise the narrative independence of each of the episodes which make them up, yet because of the care with which they are arranged in relation to one another, they instill a continuous free narration in the visitor.

Consequently when it came to discussing city projects, each building could become a pavilion in itself by assuming a fictional status with which to cloak its actual function. The way it looked could be inscribed with overt pathos, the way it worked could adopt a ready choreographed activity. Projects had certainly begun to detach themselves from their authors in favour of a more filmic cohesion between fiction and its effect.

Cinema also began to be talked about in terms of the structure that lay behind its effect. As Eisenstein had shown, film is composed of distinct strata, such as action/movement/music/dialogue so that their assembly in experience causes an extraordinarily spatial sense of reality. Gardens too, we argued, had a similar separation of layers of meaning – dividing vistas from pathways, pathways from pavilions, pavilions from mythological inhabitants.

Around 1978, you probably listened to Talking Heads, read Artaud and wore a leather jacket because you were

Worlds End clothes in Vogue, August 1981

sick of retro clothes. People skytrained it back and forth to New York at every available opportunity, punk on both sides of the Atlantic had played out its first round. In the Soho projects, the 'sinister' theme had really taken hold. Some drawings had blizzards of black charcoal blowing across them, on occasion so dense that the buildings more or less disappeared. Other drawings amplified specified scenarios by stressing the sequential effect of moving from one space to the next. Evidently these projects enjoyed a sense of claustrophobia that grew directly out of the confinement that prisons or asylums enforce.

By the time the angry phase of punk had ended, artful underprivilege had made wealth more or less unnecessary; declining cities meant that you could invent the way to use them. Above all, you would cultivate the display side of your lifestyle. Despite all earlier warnings to the contrary, social fragmentation added a new vitality to things. Peter York identified a whole range of lifestyle groups, from *Sloane Rangers* to what he called *Postmoderns*, the type he described as 'talented, brave, working class, positive'. This new sort of young person had managed to change London's social life into an endless circuit of one-night theme clubs, like *Blitz*, the *Beat Route* or a host of others.

Although neither the Soho nor the Mayfair projects (1979-80) had been designed specifically with any of these groups in mind, they did single out particular tastes to 'narrate' each of the projects. Filling in the kinds of users and lifestyles that suited a building was a way of tightening up its fundamental need to project a sense of

the present. In addition to specified actions or users, emotions began to turn the narrative away from 'telling stories' towards the user himself creating the fictional dimension. In 1975, Bernard Tschumi had asked, in Wittgensteinian mood, 'if space is neither an external object nor an internal experience (made of impressions, sensations and feelings) are man and space inseparable?'. We decided to single out the contents of the brackets; it was the *effect* that needed to be worked on. We wanted our designing to become forthright and expressive, for the distortions of the mind to be thrown out onto the buildings so that once built, they would throw some of the same feeling back. If architecture really were to have more than a guest/host relationship with the people that filled it, it would have to anticipate the way experience constructs its own narratives, constantly superimposing logic and emotion. Architecture, we said, should define an anthropomorphic field which constantly parallels and opposes experience itself. Like life, it had to aggregate and disintegrate the experiences it contained.

This meant breaking buildings into fragments, each one wilfully interfering with all the others, so that the effect would be part cubist, part dada. Believe it or not, all the earlier experiments with the 'language' of classicism had been a useful precedent, having taught us that each bit of a building could be expanded to a fictitious scale.

Metaphors could therefore be applied to parts of the building just as well as to the whole. Every building could become a *city* of parts. . . we looked at devices which defused meanings as well as those which focused them, we began to think in terms of decoration, abstraction, of

Martin Benson, detail from the Exhibition of Architecture, 1981

colour and forms that suggest non-architectural objects. We felt inspired by fashion magazines and the NME, listed old factories as favourite buildings. We read books on the Festival of Britain, while listening to Laurie Anderson singing about the unreadability of language.

Gradually, the mix-and-match social atmosphere seemed to be finding a look of its own and nowhere was it clearer than in fashion, though not of the dictated elegance variety. In fact Peter York's 'brave, etc.' person probably dressed at Vivienne Westwood and Malcolm McLaren's *World's End* shop on the King's Road. They had managed to catch the mood of misuse. With an artful wit, Vivienne's designs distorted carefully isolated clothing conventions – jackets constructed inside out, waists too big, legs too short. Looking found rather than bought, nothing actually fitted. Which was just the effect we wanted our work to have. After all 'brave, etc.' was actually using the town around him as an experimental ground, probably because he had been thrown out into it at the age of sixteen. The landscapes of big English cities like London certainly display all the staccatoed contradictions that we were talking about, that is if you bothered to look at *everything* around you. . . railway tracks, advertising hoardings, scaffolding, old factories, traffic jams. . . as well as night-clubs, Kings Road. . . Here youth culture had become a stand-in for the avant-garde. Meanwhile, even art of the freshest kind, like the new painting from Italy or New York, had little value here. (Abroad even, it was little more than a branch of design). No, it was the way some people used cities that was art. For us to design buildings that held the same attitude was

totally natural; lots of the same 'express and pretend' techniques had already been tried. What was less clear at the beginning of the '80s was the size of the operation we were going to tackle. On one hand the scale of individual experience had become more direct, with live workshops being included in the unit's annual programme; on the other, interests had expanded to the complete urban scale. One wanted to design whole pieces of the city's terrain, *and* see what they felt like.

1980-81 was the first year this whole cycle occurred. Ricardo Pais, who had already test run a live workshop the year before, hosted the *Modern Life* project which, in the end, turned out to be a kind of performance *in camera*. Each of the students taking part developed a personal *mise-en-scène*, a particular set of movements. The real interest came with a whole room full of actions performed simultaneously, cutting into one anothers' paths. In the *Exhibition of Architecture* (1980-81's project for a sizeable chunk of the East End), exactly the same features could be found – deliberately differentiated parts extended to cut into one anothers' programmatic circuit, to create decoy meanings, and overstated movements. Even if the key narrative were the museum that people lived in, the result in urban terms was far closer to the mix of city experiences than the Barbican could ever hope for.

In many ways the *Exhibition of Architecture* had not produced anything new. Lots of its forms were deliberately chosen from world fairs or old housing handbooks. What was fresh was the intensity of the composition so that all the old signs couldn't help but cause new effects. Piles of paint and oil pastel took this assertive atmosphere even

Still from 'Pick an' Choose', video, 1981

Mark Prizeman, scene from Albion, the art/science city, 1983

further, making sure that buildings 'staged' the lives inside them.

Even if the unit had found a way of drawing to match its intentions, the project could not really escape the housing scheme formula, however many lifestyle supermarkets it had built into it. Inevitably, the next phase of things unwound the whole business of planning – it had to, if the normal use categorisations of cities were to be broken up successfully.

Giant Sized Baby Town, the unit's version of the Isle of Dogs, replaces planning with an accumulation of several narratives. The first of them is drawn out of the place itself – its barren landscapes, broken buildings and empty docks. Then a video narrative (the results of the live project run by Tony Carruthers), explores the possible mixing up of work and home without ever referring to buildings directly. Thirdly, each piece of the island (corresponding to each student in the unit) develops its own industrial process to mark a narrative of movement, process and sequence. The final narrative occurs when the experience of the place – living on the island, riding on the bus, settling into the work/home landscape – puts all these layers together. In the distorting reality that results, it is not so much a question of reading the architect's gestures in every brick or every blade of grass, but in the differential nuance that each narrative infers on any action performed in the place. Which relieves us as architects of an awful lot: narratives are no longer based on any reference to the word but on the very conditions that the place is made of, its cranes, its processes, its images. It is this spirit that the unit's recent drawings represent.

Their distorted close-ups of the city in action somehow touch the most random perceptions hidden in cursory situations, the kind of primitive freshness that architecture normally edits out. Behind them is a working process which explores ideas live, before ever putting rotring pen to drawing machine. So we work with video, with funny drawings, or with any appropriate experiment. This *narrative architecture* grows out of an elaborate combination, piling all these things on top of each other, so that in terms of actual effect, the narrative breaks up, like interference on a video screen. In the end, Giant Sized Baby Town is the place where art and architecture join. Everything you do there is touched by the resonant effects of utterly ordinary things. . . narrative break-up. . . reality becomes a screen of bursting little flares of light through which you can just make out the next episode in the unit's activity, *Albion* the art/science city threading its way from Surrey Docks across Rotherhithe and Bermondsey right up to London Bridge. ■

Jenny Lowe, They decided to knock my house down

The work illustrated here does not address itself to those looking for recipes in architectural design, for 'how-to' books offering answers to problems of composition or style. Particularly in the early years, it raised questions rather than providing answers – questions about social relevance, about architecture and ideology, about architecture and representation.

The end of the sixties, with its accompanying political upheaval, had considerably dampened the enthusiasm of those architects who thought that the alliance of architecture and technology, sociology and other related fields could provide support for their endless quest for

'Everything which used to be directly experienced has turned into à representation.' Guy Debord, opening paragraph to la Société du Spectacle, 1967

tools to 'verify where the system is going,' the early seventies at the AA clarified one other matter: metaphor was quickly discredited as the expression of obsolete contents.

Although metaphor had only begun to invade what would soon become architectural postmodernism, conversations in more experimental corners of the school, mostly around the unit, took a markedly different stance. While rejecting the

progress. The early seventies added an interest in criticism and commentary, an attempt to understand and analyse the underlying causes leading to the collapse of the architect's belief in the myths of progress. At the same time, it introduced

The unit plays on an opposition between certain political, theoretical and cri **and an art sensibility informed by contemporary photography, conceptual art an**

into the 'distance' offered by criticism new models of interpretation. One of these could be described as an ironic model. Doug Branson and Nigel Coates' project for Royal Mint Housing was purposefully processed according to the clichéd conventions of the time: urban villas, ruins and figuration, nature and the representation of order. Design was not aimed at problem-solving, but at ironically referring back to straight architectural image-making and its tragic search for a new rationality.

Besides projects developed as critical

reductionism of mainstream international style, they centred on a critique of representation, especially in the context of all-pervasive urban culture.

The work of situationists Debord and Vaneighem, Lefèbvre's texts on everyday life and 'urban revolution,' and those of their predecessors, Benjamin, Adorno and the Frankfurt School, were intensely discussed in a course of lectures. Aimed at understanding the forces acting through and on the city, it emphasised the application of political philosophy to the urban realm. Seminars were complemented by trips abroad: Paris, Florence, Turin provided a background for a series of challenges from local theorists and ideologists, while the shock value of cultural displacement accelerated invention.

At the same time, seminars with artists and art critics discussed further the representation of everyday life and its spaces. This opposition between a critical, theoretical discourse and a specifically art perspective was to characterise the unit's approach. Rosy Ind's project for a Marxist

through artificial means of representation. Although the projects illustrated in this exhibition catalogue are visual, a considerable amount of work took written or verbal form. The inherent nature of criticism, its dependence on concepts, analysis and commentary, turned the work in the direction of the texts contributed by seminar participants and students on the 'Intermediate City,' 'Cultural Dequalification,' 'Representationalism' and 'The End of Consumerism.' The ensuing

but rather with the elaboration of subjective spaces and social playgrounds. Although based on an analysis of the city in terms of social relationships and modes of production, this political journey never speaks about revolution without explicitly referring to everyday life. Refusing all constraints, its politics are not utopian in the usual meaning of the word. They are what is repeatedly being searched for in terms of practice and experience of all sorts. Their common link is that they are

Projects are as much about exploring new representational codes (such as photography) to describe new contents as about using new content to discuss the photographic mode of representation

playground functioned both as critical commentary and as a subtle exploration of a contradictory mode of representation. The surrealist overtones of her watercolours underlined her debt to situationist dialectics. Jenny Lowe, who injected invaluable vitality into the early group of staff and students, was exploring, through ritualistic performances, the immediacy of everyday experience. Her 'pieces' – at once spaces and events – were first extensively documented through photography, then reformulated by insertions of drawings and collages to provide a means of distancing representation from the reality of the original event. Nigel Coates' *Prison Park* suggested that issues judged important by previous decades might no longer be relevant. Instead of 'meaning' in the old-fashioned sense (a term attached to values), the project simply processed,

publication, entitled *A Chronicle of Urban Politics,* assumed an exploratory form in which words and images, abstractions and representations played an endless mirroring game. It reflected the spirit of a new attitude, encompassing both its weaknesses and its contradictions. Expressing a kind of architectural quest, the Chronicle's introduction suggested a new interpretation of the word 'politics':
The following journey is neither art, nor semiology, nor metaphysics, but rather politics. Not politics in the institutional sense though (Parliament, elections, parties, local authorities...) nor politics in the ideological sense (class struggle, proletariat, party...) but politics in a sense that has not yet been defined, and which perhaps must always remain undefined. Such politics are not concerned with well defined alterations to institutional rules,

considered 'non-serious'. I hope this chronicle will have the intensity of the non-serious, for example that it will be enjoyable to you.

A small publication, entitled *A Chronicle of Urban Politics,* retraces the students' itinerary through texts and images on fragmentation, cultural dequalification and representation

programmatically and formally, ambiguous material through the apparently objective photographic mode.

Much of the work was caught in conscious and unconscious contradictions. It hinted at everyday life while occluding it, first through distancing rituals, then

ncerns
mance

Marxist Playground

Rosemary Ind

The title is not, and never was, correct but refers to a response to the situationists in Paris, 1968, and to the work of Henri Lefèbvre.

It will be noticed that seeds of another reverse are implicit in some of the statements within the work, e.g. Marx/Nero fiddles while London burns. When I could have been learning how to build I was making rhetorical comments.

What I now think should be détourné is the chance to act. Every building designed by a half awake 'architect' is a chance lost. Along the Pataphysical Promenade, which can now perhaps be designed, are seats where you can rest and think; seats in space, cold seats, windy seats, hard seats, wobbly seats, seats under trees, shared seats. If Klee was talking about the Thinking Eye, architects should be talking about the Thinking Body. Orpheus emerges as the new hero, who sings his song in full knowledge that winter will come, and go.

Seat for Newton/Prometheus

I propose a Pataphysical Promenade with seats, to gratify the senses and attack sensibilities...a reserve for experimental capable amateurs and innovators who will be needed when the Empire falls

Marxist Playground, 1974, ink and watercolour on paper

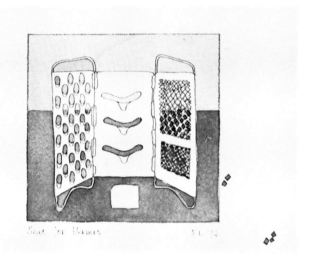

Seat for Hermes   R.L. '74

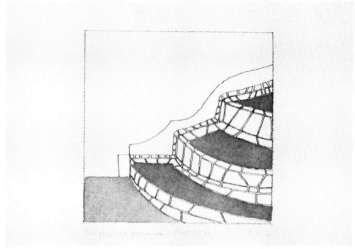

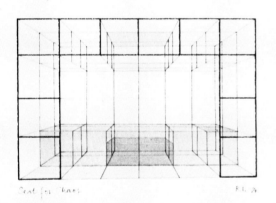

Seat for Chaos   R.L. '74

Seat for Orpheus   R.L. '76

Prison Park

Nigel Coates

Within the gardens the following acts are prohibited:

Permitting any animal to be in any boat.

Failure by any person having charge of any animal to remove it from the Gardens on being requested by a Park Keeper or Police Constable to do so.

Wilfully disturbing or injuring any animal, fish or bird or taking any egg.

Wilfully interfering with the comfort or convenience of any person in the Gardens.

Collecting or soliciting money.

Dropping or leaving litter except in a receptacle provided for the purpose.

Any act which pollutes or is likely to pollute any water.

Climbing trees or railings, fences or structures of any other kind.

Playing any game or engaging in any form of sport or exercise after being requested by a Park Keeper or Police Constable not to do so.

Using any mechanically propelled or operated model after being requested by a Park Keeper or Police Constable not to do so.

Sailing model boats except on the Round Pond.

Behaving or being clothed in any way reasonably likely to offend against public decency.

Bathing.

Boating a) in any area enclosed for any purpose or b) except at a time when boating is permitted by notice or sign exhibited by order of the Minister.

Embarking or disembarking from a boat elsewhere than at a place appointed by a Minister for that purpose.

Making use of a playground by persons other than boys under 13 years of age and girls under 15 years of age.

Breaking or damaging any ice, throwing things upon it or any other act in relation to it which is likely to interfere with the safety or convenience of skaters.

Behaviour (including the use of words) which is in any way likely to cause disorder or breach of the peace.

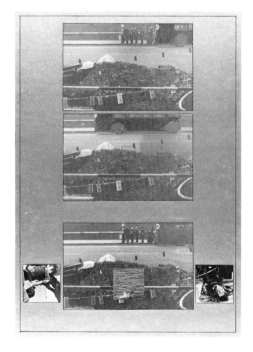 

Any person who has contravened any of the Regulations shall, on demand by a Park Keeper or a Police Constable, give his name and address

Prison Park, 1974, mixed media and photographs on board

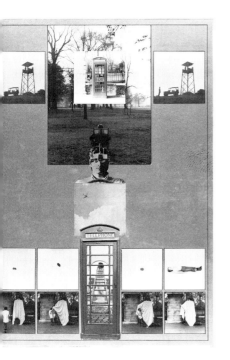
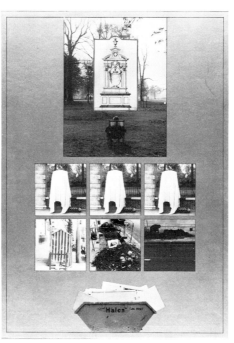

Five Spaces

Jenny Lowe

Ten years ago one would speak of the 'I', of the individual, subjecting one's life to architectural situations, to real-space intentions, for the purpose of extracting criteria with which to design. Then, any trace of clichéd values or dogmatic rules were viewed with great suspicion. Perhaps this was the aftermath of 1968.

In 1974, when *Five spaces* was done what remained of the avant-garde still heatedly opposed itself to the urban rationalists who were writing books of rules for the ways one could intervene upon the city.

Today this opposition, for the convenience of clarity or dialogues, is cited as being between the classicists and the modernists. This opposition is not stylistic as such. It depends more on the way in which an architect addresses the present — if the spirit of the classicist appears to be one of consolidation, of earthbound rules that protect contemporary uncertainties and eternal aspiration, the 'ism' of modernism suddenly becomes very appealing.

In 1917, Victor Shklovsky described the purpose of art as 'awakening the sensation of life'. He discussed devices which included the de-familiarisation of habitation. Architecturally, such a sympathy makes the programme very important, with the programme being the pragmatic rules (often square meterage) which envelop our daily acts. For the art of architecture the programme becomes useful as a point of transcendence.

Yet, however skilfully and deviously one uses the programme to structure sequences of space, to layer confrontation, duration and discovery in the act of life, the problem of style somehow remains. Not style in the sense of arbitrary selection but rather how one gives expression to a contemporary spirit of optimism and belief in the possible exultation of the present.

In 1983 the discourse preferably takes place in the architectural proposition, but nostalgia remains for the passionate questioning remembered from 1974.

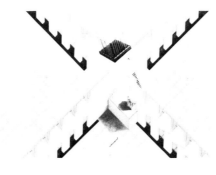

The spaces described are 'five spaces of a day'... internment, through internment, solitude, the growth of a dream, between dawn and dusk

Five Spaces of a Day, 1974, ink, pencil and collage on board

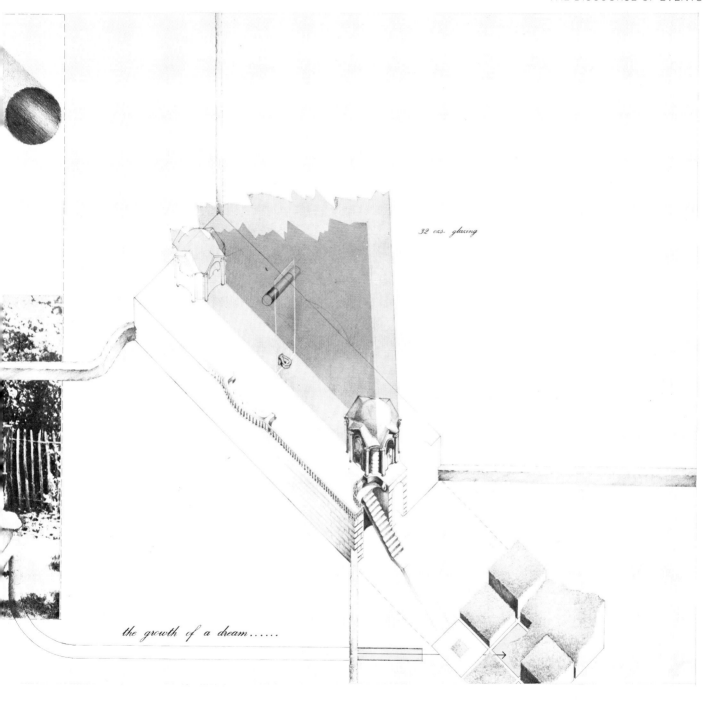

32 ozs. glazing

the growth of a dream......

Royal Mint Housing

Nigel Coates and Doug Branson

This entry for a GLC housing competition
reveals, through its visual breakdown,
some of the contradictions in government housing policy. The extending grid
of the design is in itself a statement of
prevailing attitudes to mass housing; the
buildings combine a nostalgic echo of
early 20th century utopias, with the
timeless form of the cube altered just
enough to describe a permanent state of
decomposition. Relentlessly repeating
cubes with broken corners are there, on
the ground, to dematerialise the object
ad infinitum. The two adjacent mirrored
walls of each, facing south east to catch
the light, reflect the synthetic lawn
treatment of the rear walls of
neighbouring cubes.

Only one feature attempts to break this
uniformity. Unique, destructive, the
sacred meeting between the landscape
cross and a hill, its calvary, is
immediately held up to ridicule: all it
does is point out the route to the car
park underground, and in doing so, point
out the programmes detailed idiosyn-
cracies just as clearly as do the 'five flats
per block' arrangements of the cubes
themselves.

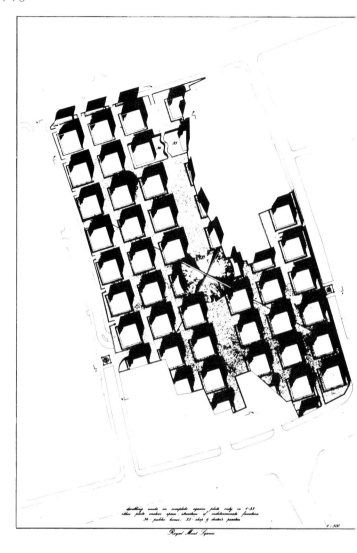

**Royal Mint Housing turns an architectural competition into a critique of conventional
architectural problem-solving and questions notions of representation and figuration**

Royal Mint Square housing competition entry, 1974, Ozalux prints

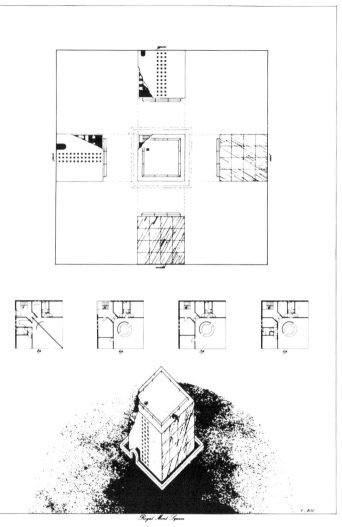

Royal Mint Square

Royal Mint Square

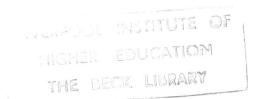

27

Joao Basto, Warehouse installation

'So I had to run with my forehead thousands and thousands of times, for whole days and nights, against the ground, and I was glad when the blood came, for that was a proof that the walls were beginning to harden.' Kafka, *The Burrow*

The Unit's Chronicles

Analysis of the city and its spectacle, and appraisal of urban theories are not in themselves informative about architectural concepts. Rather, they provide a critical framework, an objective understanding of the conditions in which work is produced, consumed, appropriated or distorted. The following projects, instead of analysing further ideological variables **The unfolding of events in a literary context inevitably suggests parallels to the unfolding of events in architecture** of architectural activity, deliberately concentrate on one constant, space, together with some of its 'literary' connotations. Such a logical shift was impelled by an attempt to develop a discourse specific to architecture. The concentration on space was aimed both at further exploring ideas discussed during the preceding year (i.e. space as a product of history) and at opposing them to specific philosophical concepts, such as the Kantian 'space as instrument of knowledge'.

Literary connotations, on the other hand,

offered a means of exploring concepts of space in other disciplines – in the arts and in literature itself. However, they also unexpectedly provided a remarkable ground for research in what was to become an obsessive theme: the relation between spaces and the events that occur within them, their relative autonomy and their conflicts. Because literature speaks, among its many subjects, of spaces, describing places, houses, landscapes and other unknown terrains, it could provide the descriptive aspect of a possible architectural programme. This representation of objects or people (the *description*) is of course juxtaposed to *narration*, the representation of actions and events. The opposition between narration and description, which is so much a part of our literary consciousness, could not fail to suggest architectural analogies. Sequences of events as opposed to sequences of spaces, architecture without events, events without architecture, strategies of reinforcement against those of disjunction became instrumental notions for several years. Kafka's *Burrow*, Borges' *Library of Babel*,

Opposing images and texts is invaluable in providing a framework for analysis of the relation between events and spaces

Hesse's *Glass Bead Game* and Calvino's *Invisible Cities* were used, not only to avoid the predetermination of an analytical brief, but to provide the necessary dialectic between an existing cultural artefact and something that could not be its mere illustration.

John Andrews' *Invisible Cities*, for example, suggested an infinite regression through which the text's subject and codes engaged in complex mutations. Joao Basto's *Library of Babel* proposed the possible necessity of a mathematical mediation between space and text. Derek Revington, by far the most adventurous, applied Hesse's *Glass Bead Game* to a year-long confrontation with the spaces of a warehouse, establishing a salutary distance between architect and text and inventing new modes of movement notation in the process.

The following quotation serves to recall something of the nature of the period's conversations. Marked by extensive attempts to find a rationale for an ambiguous territory, they suggest that architecture – not unlike art – can be successful only if it disentangles some of society's existing codes in order to invent new articulations:

Etymologically, 'defining' space means both 'making space distinct' and 'stating the precise nature of space.' Much of present confusion about space can be illustrated by this linguistic ambiguity. While art and architecture have been essentially concerned with the first sense, philosophy, mathematics, physics have historically tried to give interpretations to something variously described as 'a material thing in which all material things are located' or as 'something subjective with which the mind categorises things'. Meanwhile, and architecturally, to define

Derek Revington, Horse

space (i.e. making space distinct) literally meant 'to determine boundaries'. Despite the extended space-time concepts of the Modern Movement, the notion of space has remained simplistic, as if space were some uniformly-extended matter that could be modelled by its physical boundaries.

Questions of space: architecturally, is space the medium for the materialisation of theory?

Alkahest

Derek Revington

The founding of the City begins with ritual. The land is taken, demarcated and consecrated. It is an archetypal act signifying and evoking a new beginning. As the City grows upon itself, that original act recurs announcing its archaic origins through individual and collective works. The notations for *Alkahest* document an analogous ritual and transformation compressed in space and time.

The work attempts to extend the limits of both architectural language and methodology and to recapture that original lost sense of identity with our surroundings and with our creations, both symbolically and erotically. The score I developed for the performance observes aspects of the ancient Japanese 'Rituals of Place' and proscribes actions in space and time; the signification of territorial zones, the placing of occupation marks, the game symbols and sequences, the deployment of materials etc. It attempts to guide and facilitate while allowing the action to generate its own results in process. Uncertainty both as principle and methodology governs the work.

The photographs chronicle a narrative and act as a metronome in a space/time sequence which follows a recurring cycle of assault/uncertainty/deliberation and documentation. The notation diagrams *re*present both the alchemy and intensity of the rite, and record transformations choreographically. The photographs and plans, therefore, are concerned with space and its manipulation through time while the notation diagrams once more place the experiencing subject at the centre of the work.

Alkahest was performed in the burned out fourth floor of an empty warehouse on Butlers Wharf, Bermondsey on the 22nd of May, 1975.

A tentative, land-taking gesture. Round and round, moving, sensing… uncanny feelings of reference…

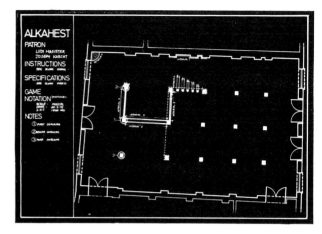

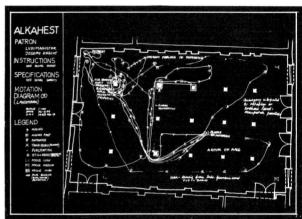

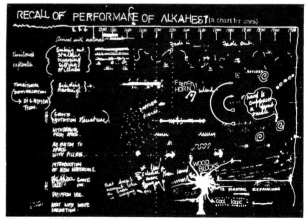

Alkahest, 1975, reversed ink drawings/performance

The Library of Babel

Joao Basto

'The library exists *ab aeterno*. This truth, whose immediate corollary is the future eternity of the world, cannot be placed in doubt by any reasonable mind. Man, the imperfect librarian, may be the product of chance or of malevolent demiurgi; the universe, with its elegant endowment of shelves, of enigmatical volumes, of inexhaustable stairways for the traveller and latrines for the seated librarian, can only be the work of a god. To perceive the distance between the divine and the human, it is enough to compare these crude wavering symbols which my fallible hand scrawls on the cover of a book, with the organic letters inside: punctual, delicate, perfectly black, inimitably symmetrical'.

J.L. Borges *The Library of Babel*

...an indefinite, perhaps an infinite number of hexagonal galleries, with enormous air shafts between

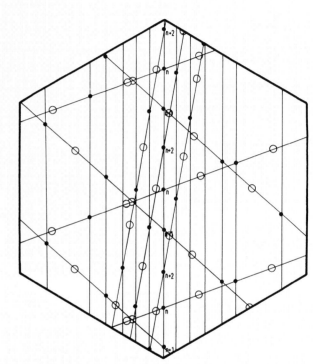

— corridors
• spiral stairc.
○ hexagonal galler.

SPATIAL REPRESENTATION

The Library of Babel, 1975, ink and crayon with tracing overlays

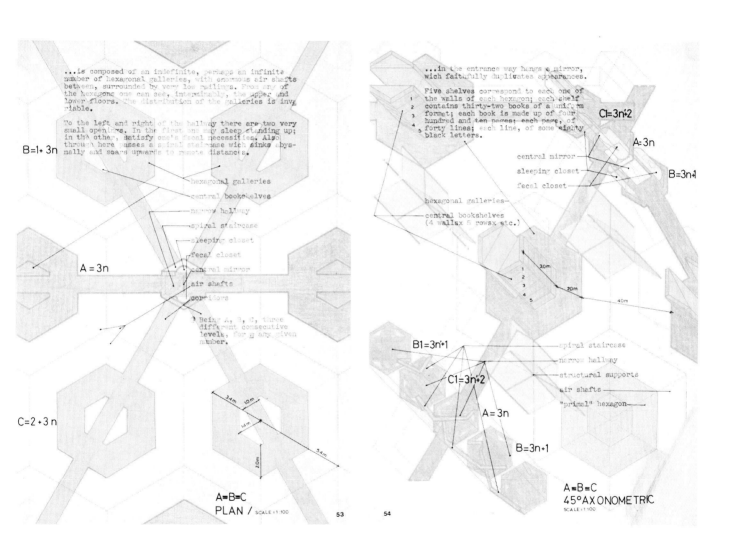

...is composed of an indefinite, perhaps an infinite number of hexagonal galleries, with enormous air shafts between, surrounded by very low railings. From any of the hexagons one can see, interminably, the upper and lower floors. The distribution of the galleries is invariable.

To the left and right of the hallway there are two very small openings. In the first one may sleep standing up; in the other, satisfy one's faecal necessities. Also through here passes a spiral staircase wich sinks abysmally and soars upwards to remote distances.

B=1+3n

A = 3n

C=2+3n

hexagonal galleries
central bookshelves
narrow hallway
spiral staircase
sleeping closet
fecal closet
central mirror
air shafts
corridors

Being A, B, C, three different consecutive levels, for n any given number.

A=B=C
PLAN / SCALE 1:100

53

54

...in the entrance way hangs a mirror, wich faithfully duplicates appearances.

Five shelves correspond to each one of the walls of each hexagon; each shelf contains thirty-two books of a uniform format; each book is made up of four hundred and ten pages; each page, of forty lines; each line, of some eighty black letters.

C1=3n+2

A=3n

B=3n+1

central mirror
sleeping closet
fecal closet

hexagonal galleries
central bookshelves
(4 wallsx 5 rowsx etc.)

B1=3n+1

C1=3n+2

A = 3n

B=3n+1

spiral staircase
narrow hallway
structural supports
air shafts
"primal" hexagon

A=B=C
45°AXONOMETRIC
SCALE 1:100

33

The Light Box

Doug Branson

I wanted to experiment with the concept of physical work, to produce a three-dimensional piece which...

destroys an existing space by breaking down familiar patterns of meaning given to spaces; exchanges the roles of observer and observed, thus contradicting the subject-object relationship; has imposed on it spatial information which is unpredictable and defies categorisation; emphasises the role of the observer in forming an object.

A specific room was chosen (any space would be suitable), its normal use noted but denied consequence. The room was blacked out, eliminating the existing awareness of space and meanings given to it. Luminous tapes were attached to its extremities, transferring the function of memory from the person to the room itself. A number of white lights were distributed randomly throughout the space (white light was presented as having no value or meaning in itself).

Is the experience of space the experience of the materialisation of the concept of space?

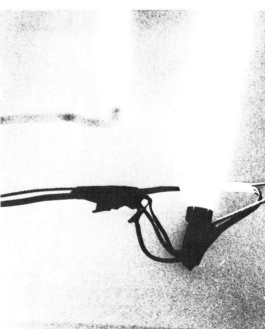

The Light Room, 1975, installation

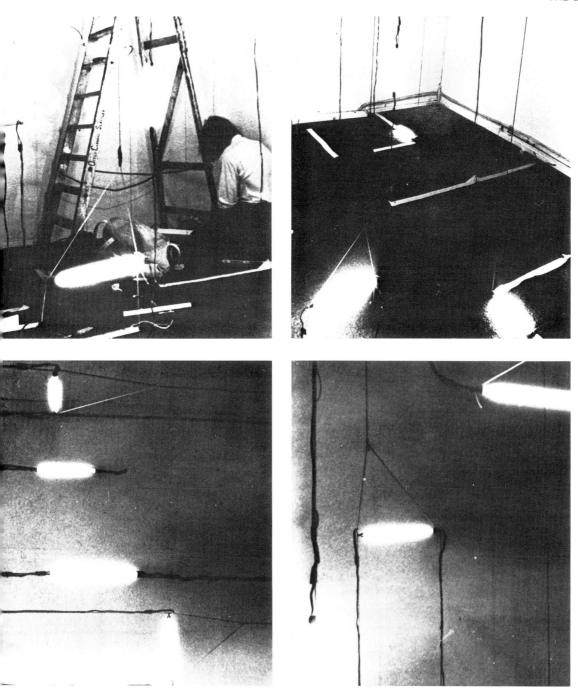

Fendora

John Andrews

"MARCO POLO: 'Perhaps this city exists
in the shadow of our lowered eyelids.
But each time we half close our eyes, in
the midst of the din and throng, we are
allowed to withdraw here, dressed in silk
kimonos, ponder what we are seeing
and living, to draw conclusions, to con-
template from the distance.'
KUBLAI KHAN: 'Perhaps this dialogue of
ours is taking place between two
beggars nicknamed Kublai Khan and
Marco Polo, as they sift through the
rubbish heap, piling up rusted flotsam,
scraps of cloth, wastepaper. While drunk
on the few sips of bad wine, they see all
the treasures of the east shine around
them."   Italo Calvino *Invisible Cities*

ANOTHER: 'I had always believed
Fendora to be a banished city, its people
never showing themselves except for
when they glance through the shadowy
corners or peep through the cracks in
their tungsten rooms. I once saw an
elderly Fendoran woman at the foot of
the eighty steps of Java, her face
covered by a dark netted veil. The next
moment I caught sight of a strange and
unfamiliar metal tower. In parts it had
turned to a bright ginger rust. It
dominated an area of harlequins,
elephants and mechanical birds. A light
breeze killed the stagnant air and
dislodged the grey dust from the stone
walls.'

**One historic truth is that it came from the dust of
musty silk found in recesses of the grey Fendoran stone**

Fendora, 1975, gouache on photographs and tracing print

Sometimes stories describe space, rooms, castles, cities. At other times, stories follow a plot and their narrative quality is like the successive discovery of one space after another

3

"There is another city in a city. Time never stops. Shadows always move — outside. Shadows never move — inside."
Tomoyoshi Kato

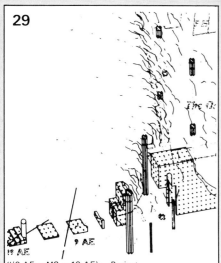

29

"(9 AE ↔ M8 ↔ 19 AE) — Project
An ideal geometrical construct is placed/materialised/distorted in Leicester Square/Covent Garden. Any reference to the other points in the area is carried through 'objects' (groups of columns, memory map)."
Hans Hiegel

After a two year break from the AA, the unit reformed as a special project option in the summer term of 1977. The *Joyce's Garden* project, organised in conjunction with various Diploma School units, was a quick incursion into the literary world. James Joyce's *Finnegan's Wake* provided the 'brief', much of the theory, and a reminder about attitudes at times of cultural or social change. Covent Garden provided the ground, the spatial experiences, the wit and the fantasies. Much of the project was set against a background of questions *vis-à-vis* the prevailing nostalgia for architectural order. It also aimed at exploring a multitude of urban and literary obsessions.

Excerpt from *Joyce's Garden* brief:
Sometimes 'stories' describe spaces, *rooms, castles, cities. So, for example, the biblical Tower of Babel becomes the origin of countless visual representations. At other times stories follow a plot, and their narrative quality is like the successive discovery of one 'space' after another. So the rituals of the Free Masons generate the successive rooms of their lodges. Sometimes stories deal with metaphors of all sorts. Ideal cities become the symbol of new orders, or Terragni's Danteum turns into an elaborate reference to the complexities of The Divine Comedy. But when texts have no narrative framework, when all is distorted and apparently arbitrary, what happens?*
Joyce's words are compressed ('Auto-binotons...'), words are grouped ('deesperation of deispiration at the

diasporation of his diesparation...'), additional phrases are inserted to thicken the basic ideas. It must be read over a period of time. Like architecture. You can never get it all at once. Is Joyce's work about the dissolution of time a conventional narrative logic? And is any architectural discussion which refers to Joyce a challenge to most architectural dogmas?

Joyce adopted the technique of getting the book's major figures and motifs on paper as quickly as possible, feeling that these were, 'not fragments but active elements' which would, 'begin to fuse of themselves' in time. His favourite analogy for this mode of composition was that of an engineer boring into a mountain from different sides, 'I want to get as many sketches done or get as many boring parties at work as possible...'

Covent Garden is not Joyce's Dublin. But it is a characteristic and well-defined urban area. It has a long, adventurous, and contradictory history, from the nuns to the cabbies, from the actors to the property tycoons, Royal Operas and historic

9

Batsheva Ronen

Rot a speck of pa's malt had Jhem or Shen brewed by arclight and rory end to the regginbrow was to be seen ringsome on the aquaface

underground, masonic lodges and floral pavilion, 'Rules' and the Salvation Army, the Strand and the Lyceum, the Churches and the Roxy. Things there dissolve and clash already. All that was 'wanted' was some intensification, identification, imagifi-

22

"(...) To introduce in a bookform an overriding "intellectual" order aimed at replacing things or experiences which cannot be codified means either to destroy them or to reduce them to metaphors."
Rodney Place

cation, absurdification?

The text itself was the brief. But instead of suggesting rooms, corridors, streets, squares or their respective sizes and functions, this brief suggested how these elements *related* to one another. It may have had something to do with a story (somebody's wake), but really what counted was the *handling* of the story, not the story itself. It had to do with how activities form, inform, deform and misform spaces. And vice-versa, of course.

Neither was the *urban* character of the project to be neglected. The games played with words could certainly find their equivalent in the design of a room, for a bit of urban perversity may have complex charms which a single room often ignores.

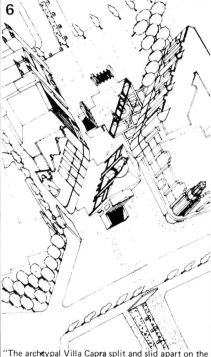

"The archetypal Villa Capra split and slid apart on the diagonal qualifies a new London Square. Two existing blocks remain within the 'square'. The two halves of the Rotunda play on the tension with the surrounding spaces. The site opens out to a formal hard-surfaced court to the north and a grassed axial approach to the villa in the south."
Sandra Honey

6

Finnegan's Wake **becomes the programme, Covent Garden the site The architecture derives, by analogy or opposition, from Joyce's text**

The locations were merely a technicality in order to facilitate both the choice of a site and the relationship between the contributors. Students were invited to choose any one point nearest any place they particularly wanted to handle in the Covent Garden area. The 36 locations were placed according to the random logic of an ordinance survey grid, nothing else.

Joyce's Garden

From the beginning of *Finnegan's Wake*: *riverrun, past Eve and Adam's, from swerve of shore to bend of bay, brings us by a commodius vicus of recirculation back to Howth Castle and Environs. Sir Tristram, violer d'amores, fr'over the short sea, had pasencore rearrived from North Armorica on this side the scraggy isthmus of Europe Minor to wielderfight his penisolate war: nor had topsawyer's rocks by the stream Oconee exaggerated themselse to Laurens County's gorgios while they went doublin their mumper all the time: nor avoice from afire bellowsed mishe mishe to tauftauf thuartpeatrick: not yet, though venissoon after, had a kidscad buttended a bland old isaac: not yet, though all's fair in vanessy, were sosie sesthers wroth with twone nathandjoe. Rot a peck of pa's malt had Jhem or Shen brewed by arclight and rory end to the regginbrow was to be seen ringsome on the aquaface.*

2 Will Alsop
3 Tomoyoshi Kato
6 Sandra Honey
9 Batshava Ronen
10 Fred Scott
15 Philip Malcomson
19 Nigel Coates
22 Rodney Place
23 Besse Hatz
24 Al Levitsky
29 Hans Hiegel
31 Iolanda Stranescu
33 Ann Sachs
36 Bernard Tschumi

Typologies, mythologies, spatial compressions, logical constructions, all dissolve. Inarticulated forms collide in a staged and necessary conflict: repetition, discontinuity, quotes, clichés and neologisms

Joyce's Garden, 1977, Projects superimposed on Ordinance Survey

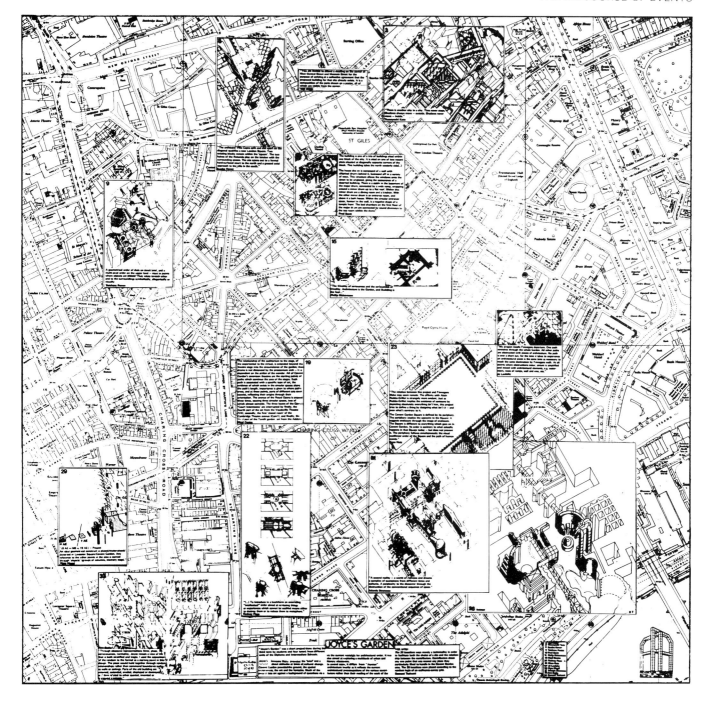

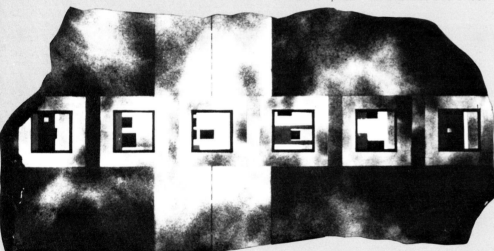

Layering, juxtaposition and superimposition of images intentionally blur the conventions afforded by plans, sections and elevations

Literary parallels, formal transformations applied to words and sentences, and the distancing such manipulation offered ('the autonomy of form') all announced the existence of a disjunction between space and events. This disjunction suggested that there was no clearly decipherable relation between architecture and programme, that doctrines of functionalism, in their emphasis on a cause-and-effect framework for research. These oppositions were programmatic content and urban typology, urban typology and spatial experience, spatial experience and procedure, procedure and building type, building type and spatial sequence, spatial sequence and urban typology. The constant element within these organised tensions was the role played by events in the organisations of spaces. Typologies, for example, were used as a rational background for a series of intangible and disturbing factors, factors which would ultimately alter the nature of the typologies. To single out particular areas of concern, such as the rational play of language as opposed to the experience of the senses, would have been a tedious game, had it been directed towards a naive confrontation of opposites. Warnings were thus inserted into the year's briefs:

Purely visual or formal solutions will not be accepted unless they correspond to an explicit wish to transcend all functions and

Chris Macdonald, *Made in New York*

relationship between function and form, had been misleading. If there were no direct causality between spaces and events, perhaps such disjunction could be

Movement notation derived from choreography, scores derived from music notation are transposed for architectural purposes

further explored in other aspects of architectural thinking.

Six particular oppositions were analysed during the year and emphasised in a corresponding project. The set of oppositions did not entirely determine the nature of the project but provided a general

symbols into a scenario, a timetable or a set of regulations.

Emphasis on programmes began to suggest an attenuated form of architectural melodrama: *Heartbreak Hotel* (which opposed its programme to a strict crescent typology), *The Opera and its*

Double (contrasting procedure and building type, and relying heavily on Artaud's writings), *A Tall Building, near a River, with a Plot* (opposing building type and vertical spatial sequences). Yet events had no rhetorical priority; they were simply presented as part of the subject matter. An occasional commitment to eccentricity would present some aspect in abrupt isolation, as in John Ryba's *Embankment Changing Rooms* with their exacerbated presentation of the architect as alienated subject of his architecture. In contrast, Chris Macdonald's *Embrace* suggests that the architect becomes both *metteur-en-scène* of, and voyeur to, a dramatic encounter, but is left holding a fragment of action rather than a full scenario.

Key to the developments of such programmatic strategies was the idea of notation. The insertion of programmatic elements, movements or events implied breaking down some of the traditional components of architecture. Scores, such as John Perver's *Theatre of Restriction*, indicated that such deconstruction permitted an independent manipulation of each part according to any narrative or formal considerations (just as the violin could be made independent from the piano in a concerto). They also suggested that juxtaposition of spaces and events could lead to their drawn superimposition – to a layering of multiple interpretations against

a layering of representational codes (text, drawings, photographs).

At the end of the year, the unit announced its manifesto. It was somewhat heroically rhetorical, but it was the expression of new certainties. Used as the introduction outlining the various unit programmes, it read as follows:

The object of the unit is to develop experimental and polemical schemes which will explicitly contribute to the making of a new pleasure of architecture. The unit advocates conceptual and formal sophistication as well as uninhibited architectural proficiency. It encourages new sensiti-

New modes of notation are devised whenever conventional plans and sections do not suffice to elaborate architectural ideas

vities – both in terms of art and/or ideas –yet it unashamedly seeks to give 'architectural' form to contemporary attitudes towards urban life, its excesses and its delights.

It is deeply suspicious of the notion that the architecture of cities can be improved by finding a formula for progress. It rejects as arrogant the idea of 'enlightenment' that has dominated architecture (likewise politics or culture) for so long. It intends to go beyond the simplistic debates of the past decades – modern versus historical, purist versus inclusivist – by encouraging

imagination and original work rather than fancy, flatly rhetorical pieces where nostalgic snatches of all sorts of architecture are knitted together in the service of campy neo-Victorianism or neo-purism.

The unit strongly insists on projects spanning conceptual aspects of architecture as well as its more experiential aspects. Each of these projects has a strong urban bias in terms of spaces as well as of entities such as blocks, streets, crescents, embankments, parks or bridges. Minimal briefs are provided, with the understanding that they are to be extended or even transgressed.

The Large Glass

John Ryba

The project points out the impossibility of providing a single reading of the city, unless in order to take the extreme form of manifesto-like images. (Remember: any part of the city provides as many readings as there are modes of interpretation; sociological, formal, political, technological, linguistic etc.
This project combines an intentionally disruptive gesture *vis-à-vis* the city (the Wall of Changing Rooms) together with a series of autobiographical statements, introducing the notion of subjectivity into the architectural discourse.

First of all I destroyed London, then I cut it in two with a wall that ran north-south. So the people rushed towards the river only to find my walls of changing rooms lining the banks

The Large Glass, 1977, colour xerox, photography and pencil on paper

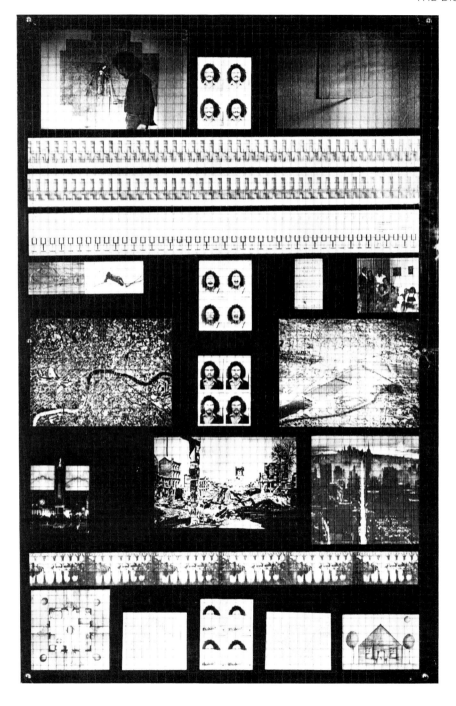

The Opera and its Double

John Perver

Conventional architectural drawings often lead to a compartmentalised and broken series of visions with reliance on a verbal explanation to tie the sheets of drawings into one coherent vision. In contrast, architectural notation is syncretic and its aspirations are in direct opposition to the architectural drawing. To some extent, it burdens the drawings in favour of self-explanation and self-reference; notation imprints the voice of the architect, so offering a text which reads with familiarity of the 'author'.

The project illustrated here, 'The Theatre of Restriction', reveals a series of parts and their operation. The multiplicity of information, written (language), orchestration (specific instrumentation and notation), site and spatial arrangement, as well as spatial and figurative directives all suggest the hyperbolic experience of opera and its reciprocal — the city.

The 'building' itself is open to the elements, circular in shape, bounded by an integral undulating path. Visual restriction imposed on the audience necessitates a corresponding movement to find an adequate view; walls, floorspace and a path providing varying degrees of visibility.

Movement notation is there to recall that architecture is also about the movement of bodies in space

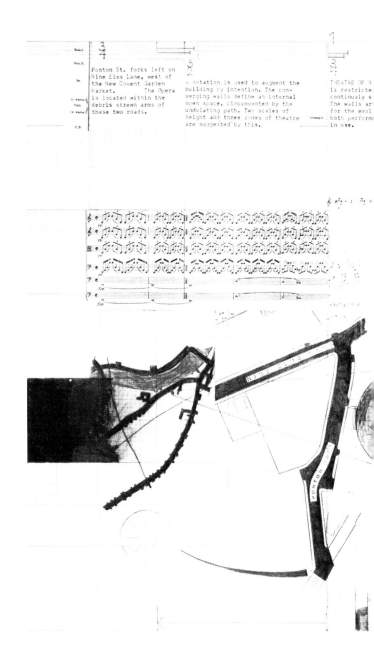

The Opera and its Double, 1978, pencil and ink on paper

Veiwing

areas which the audience
o the musicians and performers.
fore define precise vistas
hree zones are the domain of
but for the walled stage areas

During the movement and interval the audience
use the path suggestive of the rollercoaster
movement of height x time x distance. Music
reinforces the suggestion still further and
carries into the 2nd. Movement. When the
action is located the zones are known.

2nd Movement. The perimeter wall becomes the
means for an alternative escape of action and
final reunion off stage.

The 2nd Movement merges with the 3rd,
over the 4 minuits break. The Opera
climaxes towards the centre of the stage.

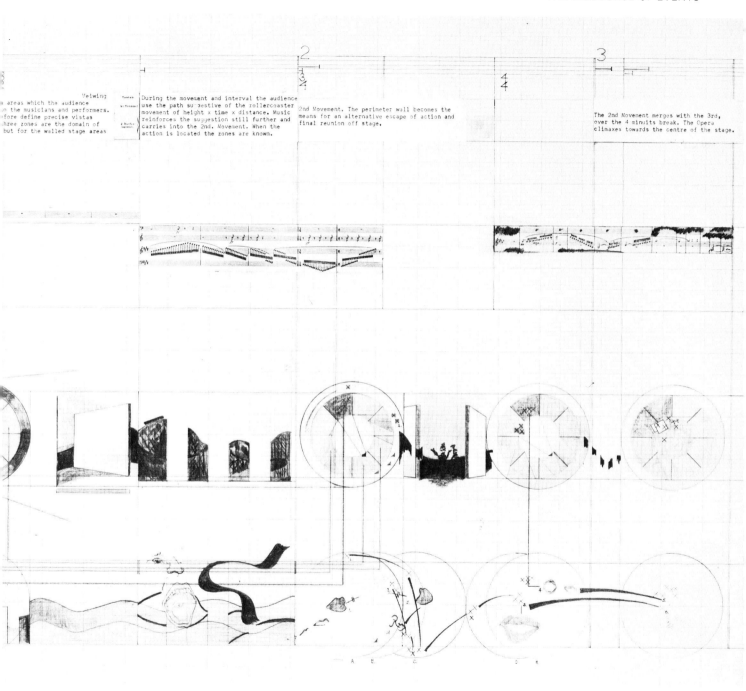

A Tall Building

Murray John

'Chelsea roundabout' is a project for a tall building of eighteen dwellings. In groupings of six, it covers three patches of waste ground where river, canal and garden are divided by the junction of Chelsea Bridge Road and the Embankment. I chose the site for the provocative qualities of the neglected ground behind the walls. Discreet gardens were seen as auditoriums, and the elements around the site as appropriate characters in three Greek myths. The atmosphere of the spaces grew from the ideas in the plays. Each apartment consists of parts of a pavilion, an outdoor terrace, rooms at ground level and a segment of an underground Pantheon. Here the river, canal and garden cascade through vaulted terraces to finally invite an introduction along riverside, towpath, and the avenues of the hospital gardens. The paper acts as a field for a three-dimensional model of limited size. I endeavoured to find a working technique which would, in the nature of the project, exclude no (possible) strains of cultural influence but show secure grounds for the selections made at any stage. My proposal works against the tendency for limited facility to produce rationalism, overt clarity or unnecessary accuracy.

The reading of the city implies a maze of references which emphasise the ambiguous relationship between concepts and experience

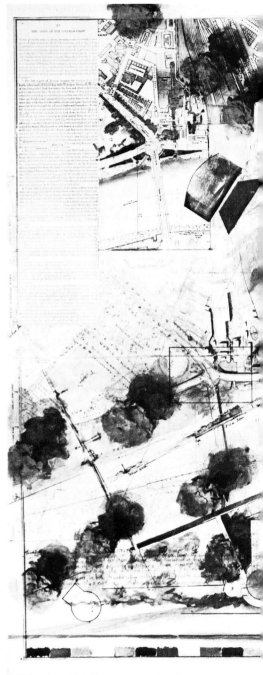

A Tall Building (Chelsea Roundabout), 1978, pencil and watercolour on paper

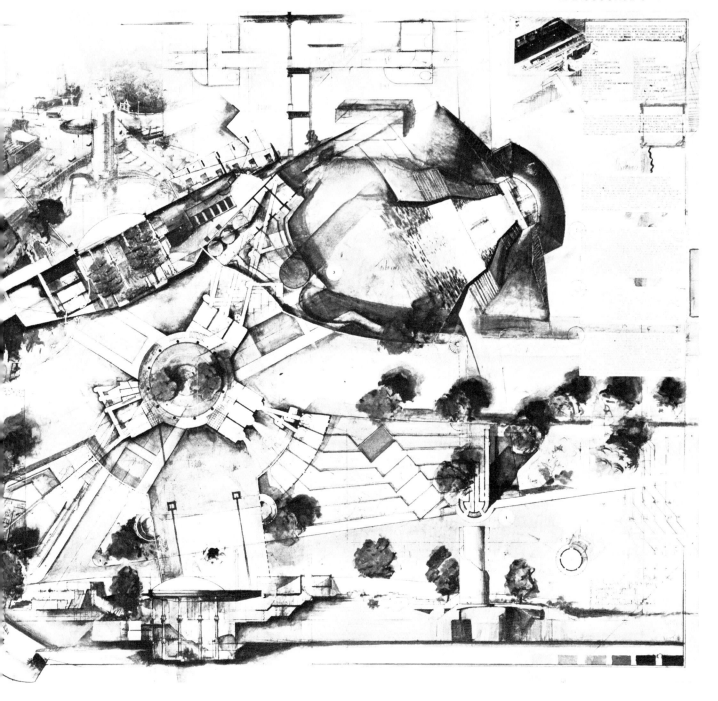

Embrace

Chris Macdonald

As with much of the work of the unit at this time, the intention to explore the periphery of 'legitimate' architecture gave rise to a deliberate rejection of many conventional formats for investigation. The project chose to harness the strength of intuitive responses to site and programme, not only to direct investigation but also to suggest the form of expression. A private logic of perception was being described simultaneous with its discovery. Coupled with a commitment to the value of the exploratory dialogue between author and paper, this has yielded images which remain, for me at least, often powerful and poignantly ambiguous. However, if viewed as tentative beginning rather than definitive conclusion, perhaps the weight of the shroud may be lifted, and the positive virtues of these studies may still be felt.

Embrace described a series of vignettes including some particular (literal) embrace, linked in motif to surroundings at various points along the embankment of the Thames. Within each scene, the capacity of a fine and subtle event to transform the perceptions of a broad and generalised space was examined, with the suggestion that 'focus' was a disproportionately significant attribute in such perception. This implicitly engaged the (then) current notion that architecture could be described as a speaking language and acknowledged a need for finesse and nuance more often consistent with reticence.

The real importance of architectural research lies in the questions it asks about the nature of architecture

Embrace, 1978, Graphite and crayon on photographs

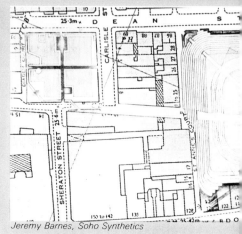

As earlier, each project displayed a strong urban bias, yet the nature of the briefs emphasised the role played by events in the organisation of spaces.

It soon became apparent that something special could be achieved by linking one project to another, both in terms of its intellectual proposition, and in terms of the ground it stood on. So while the general theme of the river had worked the

Projects opposing specific programmes with conflicting spaces explore the disjunction between expected form and expected use

year before, 1978-79 invested its operations in a relatively particular part of London, the Neal St.–Wardour St. strip through London's Soho. On it we interlocked a series of institutions, each of which represented an extreme within its (functional) type, either because of what it instituted (crime, madness) or the aberration of its context (a stadium in Soho? a ballroom in a churchyard?).

In each project (prison, stadium, asylum, ballroom) a specific building type, with a specific programme, was indicated. This emphasis on a clear programmatic choice, was reinforced by numerous historical precedents. While Michel Foucault's seminal research on asylums and prisons announced the inevitable polemic between society and the institutions of its

Jeremy Barnes, Soho Synthetics

time. Artaud's madness raised fundamental questions about spaces that set the operations of the unconscious in motion.

Police stations and prisons are extreme and generally unpopular programmatic themes. By focusing on 'discipline and punishment' the project *Police Passage (The Prison)* raised a series of uncomfortable issues on the role of the architect. If the architect is to determine the organisation of spaces, he cannot always avoid becoming a critic, a social commentator – or alternatively an apologist, a staunch

Programmatic displacement is one means of intensifying architectural effect. Shock is manufactured by the way programmes are sited in spaces

defender of disciplinary systems.

At the same time, the extreme programmatic aspects of the brief were superimposed on a specific 'passage' in London, an urban type, a long urban corridor. Many projects turned into a sharp and critical commentary, acting as 'the devil's advocate' in order to explore better the moments when architecture reaches its 'moral' limits.

A site that obviously contradicts its chosen function was presented in the project *Soho Stadium*. The sporting kind of spectacle was to be superimposed on the city as a whole. Historically, the stadium has undergone countless reformulations, both in terms of configuration, the games which it supports, and its relationship with the city itself. It was therefore not enough to design either just a building or just a game. It meant designing both a game and the urban spaces that oriented game and spectacle.

James Campbell, Soho Synthetics

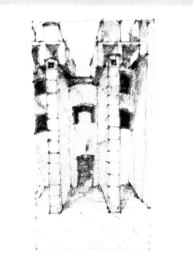

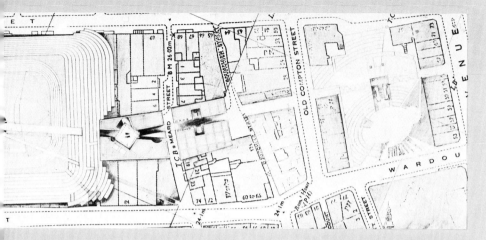

When considering the asylum (the *Carlisle Clinic*) we noted that this century, the architecture of madness has found a convenient experimental field in the cinema. The immediacy of representation, the flexibility of decors not conditioned by the large outlay of capital, has encouraged the development of haunting images. Together with the movements and preoccupations of the various protagonists, these movie spaces have provided a particular stimulus to a new vision of the world. Nature is proscribed, the mind is all powerful. 'Interior tension', 'immense accumulation of restive concentration', 'the intensive crystallisation of form' are constantly on the border of madness, as primordial anguish is only interrupted by spasmodic ecstasy. The sets of Caligari with their deliberately distorted

Soho's dense organisation of streets and squares is confronted by an array of conflicting programmes: Stadium, Prison, Asylum, Ballroom

envisaged. It is insofar as the dualities present throughout architectural theory (order versus chaos, ornament versus purity, rationality versus sensuality) generally exclude the ultimate one – reason versus madness – that a peculiar type of work needs to be done.

In the final act of confinement, on this occasion for pleasure, *Bacchantes' Ballroom* set out to explore the space of delirium and movement. The site, curious extant drama of St. Anne's, Soho, posed a bombed church and vacant lawns as a stripped paradigm for the ballroom. In this setting, the patterns and exploits of the 'crowd' cannot be separated from either the organisation or the effect of space. As observed plays against observer, space is

Michel Foucault's study on institutions provides light on the organisation of activities in buildings, whether called functions or programmes

perspectives, their inclined and dilapidated houses, the curved and slanted lines of their streets are loaded metaphysical intentions, as if oblique lines would cause different psychic reactions to straight lines.

The initial brief stated:

It should be stressed that the study of asylums and prisons is used as a means of understanding some of the attitudes that pervade the overall architectural discourse. It is insofar as architecture is the art of confinement that the most extreme cases of architectural enclosure are considered. It is insofar as architecture deals with the boundaries between the real and the imaginary that madness is

explored in complex nets of exchange in which every action enjoys a hint of the artificial, every object is, at least in part, representational.

Prison Passage

James Campbell

The combination of urban type (passage) with programme (police station) has a particular potential in Soho, an area in which conventionally forbidden pleasures are combined with commerce. In *Police Passage*, the theme of freedom of movement in conflict with the spaces of incarceration is developed literally by means of four rough-hewn timber screens. These split the passage in half along its length, separating the police station on one side from the public route on the other. Light and sound filter through gaps in the screens but movement through them is restricted. Three wings of dormitories for bachelor policemen bisect the passage/police station dividing it into a sequence of three courts. These dormitories have connotations of both imprisonment and surveillance as they bridge the passage, looking down on a street which is already notorious for its clubs and prostitution; an ironic rigidity is created through the linear arrangement of private and communal rooms, bedded into the tenements of Soho.

WARNING: Any disobedience to any of the above will mean a yellow card. A yellow card is recommended

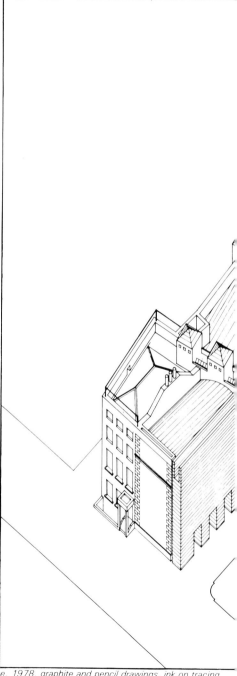

Prison Passage, 1978, graphite and pencil drawings, ink on tracing

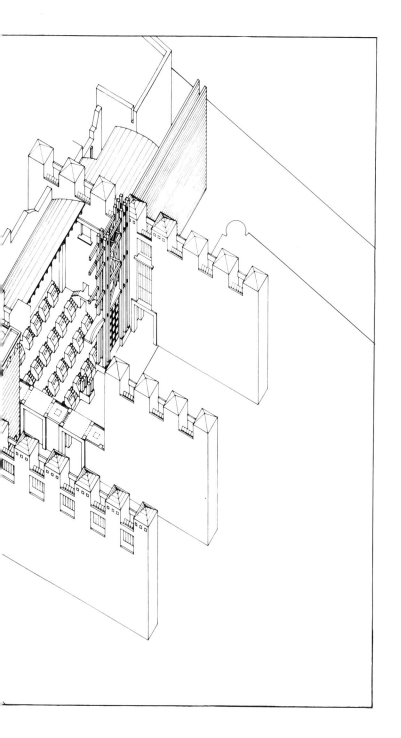

View of Screen to Cells (Passage Side)

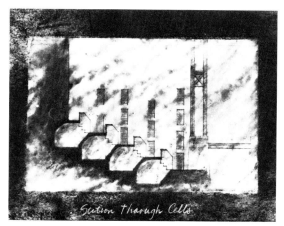

Section Through Cells

View of Screen to Booking Hall

Soho Stadium

Ron Arad

Stadiums are about obsessions. In the
stadium the masses gather to watch the
few. The masses are reduced and
multiplied individuals; the few are
individuals blown up, magnified. This is
illustrated in every football photo, in
every sports magazine. The player is
always in the foreground, huge, every
muscle, every drop of sweat showing.
The masses are in the background, an
innumerable number of coloured dots.
Every act in the arena is exaggerated in
importance and significance. The extent
to which the otherwise 'meaningless'
event (a ball touching a net or nearly
touching it) is amplified in meaning, can
be measured by the movement and
sound of the multiplied dots.

In *Soho Stadium* I wanted to emphasise
this equation of magnification vs.
multiplication. The stadium in this case is
a defined urban site. The players are its
inhabitants, its regulars. The audience
are the passersby. By introducing false
perspective, an environment that
magnifies the events in the arena and
reduces the people around it is created.
The vanishing point leads to the
continuation of the route from Meard
Street to Richmond Mews. Combining
the structure of the auditorium with its
perspectivised version on stage was a
common device in the architecture of
Baroque theatres. There, the actors had
to ensure they stood in front of the
perspectivised area; otherwise they
would have looked gigantic. I wanted my
players to look gigantic.

**The Modern Movement has experimented on the
stadium but rarely with a skill equal to that of the game**

Soho Stadium, 1978, crayon on ink drawing print

Carlisle Clinic

Jeremy Barnes

Asylum: *(as·i·lum)* sanctuary, place of refuge.

There is no collective psyche where the spirits of madmen dwell, rather their spirits have retreated to the most individual and isolated sanctuaries. The insane don't consider themselves mad. But they adhere passionately to their own logic, however hermetic the sphere of that logic may be.

This asylum has 30 hermetic cells, each the sanctuary of one psyche and mime of its madness. Each rigorously follows its own logic and, although there can be no communication between cells, there is confrontation, juxtaposition, intrusion, denial, insult.

Asylum remembers dreams.

These are extracts from the descriptive texts that accompany the drawings:

'The pneumatic couched subject is at the centre of the room. The shrill pitch of the drill returns to his ears from the smooth surface of the dome, a texture too fine to focus the upward turned eyes and thus fix its distance.'

'White ceiling, light bulb, a fine crack outlines the flush door; the spherical knob turns, the heavy door opens to reveal an identical door, a vacant keyhole, again the knob turns but this door is immovable. Light switch. Tubular steel bed frame, white pillow, grey blanket. White ceramic tiles, every one a perfect square, the floor a grey flood of carpet. Lavatory bowl. Wash basin, soap, towel, mirror.

Faint footsteps but closely, I mark the position with chalk then descend the stairs. A glance to either side tells me what I have always known. I cross the room and ascend the stairs. Still audible but receding. I mark the position with chalk.'

'The tiny weeds are plucked from the gently yielding grip of the soil. Dripping grotto, steps worn hollow, climbing, divide pristine rooms of white, deep pile wall to wall. Finally, breathlessly, dizzily to plateau of vertigo.'

For unseen judges, I move like a billiard ball across the velvet, the runner moves into a sprint, I see that his advance and mine will coincide...

Carlisle Clinic (the Asylum), 1979, pencil on paper

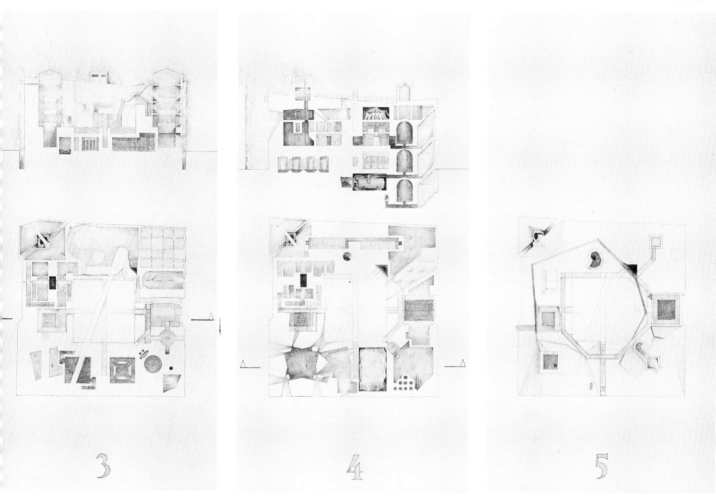

3   4   5

Carlisle Clinic

Anthony Summers

At first the public toilets off the pedestrian underpass seemed similar to countless other gestures towards the public realm of the past two decades; planning concession forced upon the developers of the Centrepoint, empty office block above. The GLC specification of mastic flooring, vandal-proof fluorescents and Ideal Standard sanitary fixtures combined with the pervasive odour of urine and disinfectant to create an atmosphere both predictable and reassuring. Thus it was with a sense of delight that he had discovered a small dimly lit marbled passage, behind a hinged false wall in one of the cubicles, the invitation of which proved irresistable. The seemingly endless passage eventually opened out into what was dimly revealed as a large flooded chamber filled with granite columns, terminating at a square platform flush to the surface of the water from which rose a steep flight of steps. In the darkness he thought he glimpsed other stairs, another passage, across the water. At the top of the steps a network of corridors at right angles to each other defined a series of rooms.

These rooms were identical apart from the occasional incongruent artifact or item of furniture. Each room, five paces square, had eight doors, two per wall, leading out into the corridors. Between the internal and external faces of each room was a narrow cavity containing two sets of steps, rising up to a gallery which circumvented the rooms. At the end of each corridor was a door. Most were false but one led to another passage. As he stepped out into the light, his memory of the space was still lucid but recollection of subsequent events was fading rapidly. Only the sharp reverberation of high heels on marble, the sound of a door latch, the cold sweat and the silence remained.

A room ... an ambiguous world, an envelope for encounters with the abnormal

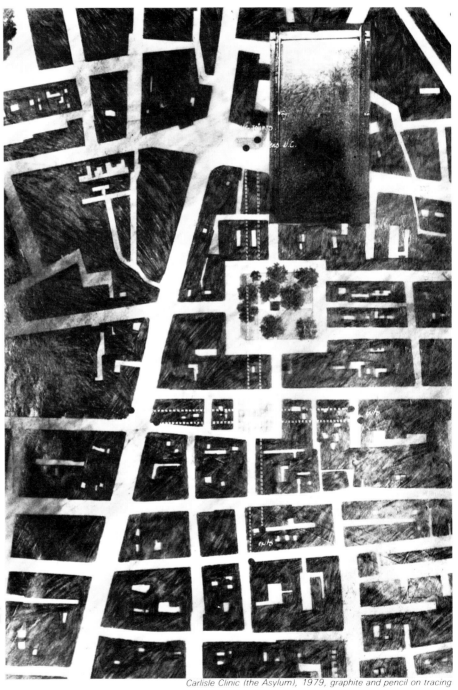

Carlisle Clinic (the Asylum), 1979, graphite and pencil on tracing

At night volumes cease to be the fact of visible walls or windows, but often depend on sound, touch or smell, and of course on a whole technology of artificial light

Night, as a narrative theme, carries through these programmes. And the spatial metaphor of the stage, 'the space of darkness', has been added to the themes of movement, sequence and notation. One talked a lot about the 'staging' of architecture, its *mise-en-scène*, about how action binds with the scene to produce effect rather than logical constructs.

One could sense that the expressive components of experience were more important than the critical ones, or as Ricardo Pais pointed out, it was time to *do* things rather than hoping to spirit them up by

talking about them.

The year focused all of its four schemes in Mayfair squares, as unwelcome visitors against the prevailing atmosphere of privilege and wealth. The *Nightclub* (the Institute of the Night), the *Vatican Embassy*, the *Fashion Institute*, deformed these squares in their particular ways, while *Singles Housing* contributed a new public space with its specified courtyard.

The first project, the *Nightclub*, invited the remaking of an existing house in Berkeley Square ('a nightingale sang. . .') into an institute for insomnia. Inside, flashing lights and darkness would alternate to blur

Stills from Airport, live workshop

Many projects wrestle with colossal volumes made from forms opposing one another like elect-rodes: the *teatri* of pure sensual space, in which fragments in motion merge with erratic pleasures

the edges of rooms, so emphasising the erotic qualities of the indistinct. We realised that an excess beyond what is functionally appropriate would make signs more volatile.

Following the *Nightclub*, Ricardo Pais conducted a theatre workshop in which the potential of a particular studio room

humanitarianism brought out the monumental tendencies of Grosvenor Square even more than the existing American Embassy. Occupying the middle of its patch of countryside, it would form its own calvary of 20th century ecclesiastical reform, in the face of the other embassies staring at it from the edges of its lawn.

Hanover Square hosted new offices for *Harper's & Queen*, in the form of a fashion institute. It suggested that the impact of the magazine page would spread out into new fashion events and gestures, this time converting the picturesque into the socially dynamic; the permanence of the architectural icon would emphasise the speed of the city as a system of constant motion and constant exchange.

Where would the protagonists of the previous projects actually live, indeed what kind of people would they actually

We will seek all opportunities to 'play up' the occasions which reinforce or intensify the quality of spaces. Reciprocally, we will analyse how these spaces can reinforce or modify the nature of particular activities

was explored with the language of movement, the body rather than the pencil. Four phases of the night (expectation, excitement, deception and tedium) were selected as distortion devices to use against the 'airport', the situation theme of the whole piece. The half hour performance which resulted, inserted moments of horror or tension into elaborate scenes of repetition built around the act of 'checking-in'.

The Pope's jet tour to Ireland and the U.S. raised ambiguities of architectural power. We said, 'on the one hand, an Embassy must be a portrait of the state it represents, and on the other, be an effective defendable compound'. The obsession of the Vatican for a sympathetically modern

be? Unconcerned with family issues, they were probably single, and ready for intriguing social opportunities. So Mayfair yielded its final proposition, the fourth and final square, with a new kind of private space around the edges, and a new monument in the centre. The irregularity of the rooms would be levelled by the monumental image through the windows.

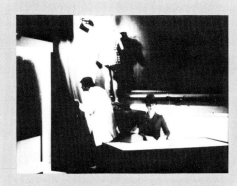

The Vatican Embassy

Jeremy Barnes

The project considers the fiction of Britain becoming a Catholic Nation. So, Grosvenor Square is terraced to accommodate huge crowds before the embassy building. The terraces contain crowd control and surveillance points in concealed, defensible bunkers, whereas the embassy building adds the image of the fortress to its more obvious stately, propagandist and religious functions. At off-peak times, the terraces work as an enormous outdoor fitness centre, so combining fitness of the body with health of the mind.

'Seven hundred and ten million catholics today took part in a worldwide simultaneous mass. This most recent event in the current explosion of public support for the Vatican's hard line, but popular, policies was the culmination of months of well-attended, open air events all over the globe. The Pope has succeeded in rallying together the Catholic world by his personal appearances (one half of Ireland's Catholic population saw the Pope in person); by relaying these events by satellite, an estimated 710 million Catholics joined in a transcendental alliance.'

'Thousands pressed forward on the stepped terraces of Grosvenor Square. As always, Vatican Guardsmen masked their insidious presence by keeping a low profile in their subterranean hideouts. . . on the video screens, the Ambassador's arm raised to bless the congregation. As he did so, his sleeve slid down his forearm to reveal a sophisticated timepiece. . .'

Despite the locked doors beneath the Papal Arms' crossed keys, the building will reflect both splendorous support *and* hard edged dissent

Vatican Embassy, 1980, pencil and xerox on pa

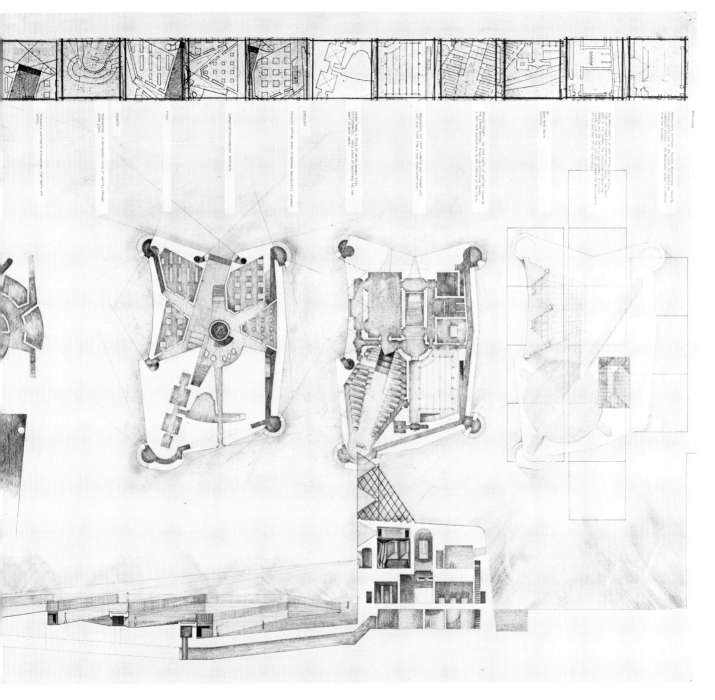

Singles Housing

Lisette Khalastchi

In the heart of Mayfair, touching the transient hotel population on one side, and Shepheard Market on the other, is a refuge for the single person, the city nomad. It can be entered on four sides, each entrance acting as a different filter from the city, each determining the perception of the central space. This is enclosed by four communal towers at the corners, anchors to the existing network of streets, and on the sides by four blocks of single rooms.

All the rooms, whether single or collective, enforce the tension between enclosure, whereby the single is hyper-aware of his individuality, and connection, where he feels part of a larger group.

From within the single room, the connecting balconies and entrances are constant invitations to break the hermetic quality of the cell. The communal towers, spacious, gentle, sloping staircases with niches in heavy walls cylindrical baths with changing cubicles, the garden with its vertical walks – all offer invitations for personal habitation for a minute, an hour, or even a few days. The central space is itself a celebration of movement with its circular car ramp extending down into the ground and rotating ballroom on the roof. In contrast, the crowning cornice contains a running track only wide enough for the solitary long distance runner to look down on the city.

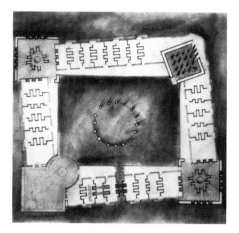

The manipulation of designed space depends more on the deformation of acute spatial elements than on the adoption of straight-forward typology

Singles Housing, 1980, graphite and pencil on tracing

Singles Housing

Karen Wainer

Housing for single people at the intersection between Broadway and Sixth Avenue in New York: autobiographical note or blue print for a meeting with the mountain carved by glass blades, in which everything appears to be numbly consumed.

A square, still containing remnants of rock of the original, amorphous landscape from which it was formed, acts as a residual void between the bisecting lines of the rational grid of the city.

The rock protruding from the grating cast over it, is dissected by a wall which parallels the asymmetrical line of Broadway, running against the grain of the grid and terminating at the point of ascension (the lift shaft). The four lines projecting upwards accommodate: the *backdrop*, an existing building (high rise car park and hostel); the *department store*; the *apartment block* for single people (at its peak, the mountain crest and glass blades); the *facades* of the two buildings and the *gateway* to the square, containing fragments of the various forms of the sliced mountain. Execution of the work and its subject are one entity; after laying bare the square and the rock in the dusty grey plain at ground floor level, the crystalline structures are erected. Singular objects are exhibited within the clinical interior of the department store, while in the apartment block, dwellings have to be carved out between floors which no longer lie parallel to the face of the earth, and glass walls which offer no privacy.

Night spaces correspond to the most *ideal* part of architecture, the architecture that literally cannot be seen, a kind of conceptual statement that coincides with its physical reality

Singles Housing, 1980, ink, pencil and acrylic on tracing

Features like the Skylon seemed to float, while the dome of discovery had apparently just landed

By this time the unit no longer structured its year by working through a series of independent set pieces tied only by virtue of a manifold attitude. Each project would set the pretext for the next, so that towards the end of the year an enormous

Programmes will explore an attitude to design in parallel with the most intense of contemporary issues, its crises, its fads and its transgressions

Stills from Modern Life, live workshop

range of visual fragments would have been manipulated from many points of view. It seemed that in the past too much time had been spent dwelling on other creative fields – writing, art or film. The time had come to experiment with the interface between architecture and everything that filled it up – with buildings and the lifestyles they contained. Instead of looking at hallowed models, we worked with the down-and-out side of cities. The city itself seemed to provide far more than vacant plots on which to site imaginary buildings. We used a second Ricardo Pais workshop to make the *dependence* of architecture more apparent by acting it out. Then we continued the process with the design of a complete new section of the East End.

In an attempt to start with the crises, the year's cycle of four projects began with

unemployment. Right in the heart of the City of London, under the shadow of St. Paul's, a small Wren church called *St. Andrew's by the Wardrobe* was chosen as the site for the first project. As the proposal was to convert it into an employment exchange, only the carcass and tower of the church was to be retained. Inside, the *St. Andrew's Exchange* would function like any of its sister offices, but in addition, dramatise the whole business of signing on and collecting one's money.

Euphemistically entitled *Modern Life in the*

City, the live workshop asked for each student to dream up and then perform a 'modern situation'.

The point of the project was twofold: firstly, to discover the spatial significance of the situations by describing them with performed actions instead of drawings, and secondly, to translate each of these pieces into a design for a public space.

One knew that the movements could not be translated literally from room to public space. Instead, each work exploited the clash between the performance (as a score) and the inherent meanings of the site that had been chosen. The question, however, was how to make built space evoke a perceptual richness that has something to do with the circumstances of being in it. Of course, buildings cannot perform, or actually move. But they can

originally housed 1,500 people, this new project increased the population to around 5,000.

But there was more to the proposition. In 1951, as part of the Festival of Britain, the

In the past, periods of deep recession have spawned radical reappraisals of creative vocabulary
The dole queue is one of several such contemporary canons, others are violence and prostitution

contain the instigators of movement. The very permanence of architecture can only be understood with the actions that take place in it as part of its structure. Then, and only then, can architecture entertain an intimate contact with the moment of perception – of being in it, of finding that it means something.

The unit's major project, the *Exhibition of Architecture*, dealt with all of these issues at once by completely redesigning an area of East London called Lansbury. The project was to bring to the area an

intensity more characteristic of the centre of cities. Lansbury would become an urban lighthouse capable of casting its rays over East London, as the various projects for *Modern Life in the City* had done. The site, large enough almost to be a city itself, would contain the generators of its specific version of public life in addition to the more prosaic needs of housing. Whereas the 12-acre site had

site was developed as a model for the healthy new British city. Then, one would have travelled by boat from the more prestigious exhibition on the South Bank to the Lansbury Exhibition of Architecture. The publicity claimed, *'ordinary people, living in it, will be privileged to witness the newest ideas and speculations for the future being acted out before them'*. In most respects the exhibition failed to rise to these provocative claims. In other words, it provided *carte blanche* for a complete rerun.

The form of many of the year's projects grew out of exemplary moments of imagined domestic *mise-en-scène*. Fragments of daily life were taken as points of generation. Isolated incidents could then be expanded into the architectural vocabulary of each type of occupant.

Cross currents make up the corpus of contemporary attitudes: we are learning to make use of an explicit neurosis

Several projects placed great importance on open spaces of indefinite function enclosed by the buildings themselves. Hardly public spaces in the conventional sense, these were areas of collective domesticity, of promiscuity and display. Like nightclubs, they deliberately embraced and reinforced the erratic movements and intimate experiences inside them. While deliberately cut off from the outside world, they held conflicting architectural forms in tension within.

St Andrew's Exchange

Duane Van Dyke

Continuing the tradition of architecture
as a reflection of the culture in which it
was created, *St. Andrew's Exchange,* a
Wren church turned unemployment
centre, defines, manipulates, and
exaggerates the process by using
architectural devices. The elements are
all recognisable – from the institutional
glass facade to the factory cat walks,
security cameras, and video screen – but
each has taken on something of a new
life.

Unlike normal exchanges, which suggest
work to their clients with childlike job
cards, St. Andrew's builds on the
premise that jobs can be presented with
an excitement bordering on aggression.
So the pin ball environment in the King's
Wardrobe Job Centre allows scanning
the job computers or, in collaboration
with a counsellor, creation of the ideal
work situation.

For those content with compensation,
the ritual of the church and the dole
queue merge religiously; the jobless
become players in a bureaucratic
dramatisation. To create a situation in
which the unemployed are both observer
and participant, the layered cat walks are
lit in different colours for each stage.
After confronting a series of doors, initial
registration takes place in an atmosphere
of rigid definition. Thereafter, the
procedure becomes less systematized.
The choice between job centre or cash
collection must be made, the latter
requiring the negotiation of a narrow
stone stair which bursts out into the
glass cube atop the tower; here the final
expression of individuality merges with
the signing of forms. Then the descent
by a precarious open staircase to a pit
below, and finally, down the aisle to the
altar turned cashier to receive the
cheque, where security cameras
preserve and project the act for all (but
especially the recipient) in living colour.

By exploring the neurotic edge between action and deliberate style, fundamental issues will be cast in architectural roles. Drama, *mise-en-scène,* situation, constitute the rhetorical techniques of urban deformation

St. Andrew's Exchange, 1980, crayon and pencil on torn pastel paper

St Andrew's Exchange

Socrates Panayides

I decided to compress the functions of
the employment exchange into a
computer, allowing the remainder of the
building the freedom to emphasise the
actions of the claimant. Led to the
computer by a path which travels
through the converted church like a
road, he or she must then cross a bed of
sand to have his/her card punched. The
significant moment of the ritual is
reinforced by operatic singing from a
figure on a balcony above.

By simplifying habitual patterns of
activity (as is now possible via the
current technological revolution), their
significance may be expressed and
emphasised through the manipulation of
space – not to create emotions, but to
arouse those that lie hidden. For the
ultimate aim of my work is always a
humanistic one, designed to elevate the
significance *of* as well as *to* the
individual. The fact that my proposal is
for a labour exchange, rather than some
other place of public service, is not
specially important. What *is* important is
the channelling of moments to form a
total atmosphere, moments which, like
the electrical pulses in a computer, only
form meaning together.

**If you take things slowly enough, building up each movement to take possession
of a corner, or a door, or a shard of glass, watch how fast the building grows**

St. Andrew's Exchange, 1980, extracts from a series of xeroxed drawings

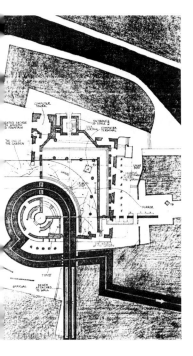
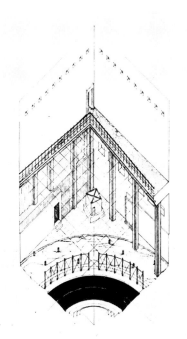
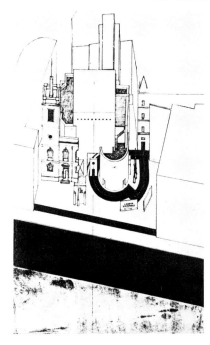
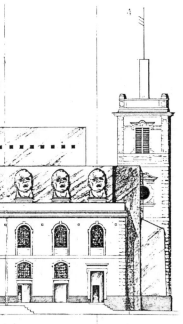

The EoA '81

Martin Benson

Suspended in a moment of time, even the domestic activity of filleting a fish could be translated into architectural form, as the series of small drawings in this project shows. I used each of the drawings to develop multiple layers of interpretation during the metamorphosis from action to architecture. Form emerges within the image, and scale within the manipulation of sequence and time. The same action can connect a cutting board, a dwelling, even a landscape.

The landscape is primarily composed of three housing types; the tower, the ditch and their logical result – the fallen tower. They mark three irregular strips across the site. Each housing type, while tending to be a reflection of its inhabitant, is formally related to the others by antithesis. The fallen towers, for example, recall the plans of the tower housing with their sections.

Between the zones of buildings, however, much wilder territory mixes the exhibition's inhabitants with the visitors. At two spots in this odd kind of urban jungle, small parts of the original 1951. exhibition of housing have been preserved, complete with their postwar tenants, as living relics.

Ultra-ordinary circumstances can be channelled into expressive dynamism

The Exhibition of Architecture, 1981, oil pastel and pencil on sugar paper

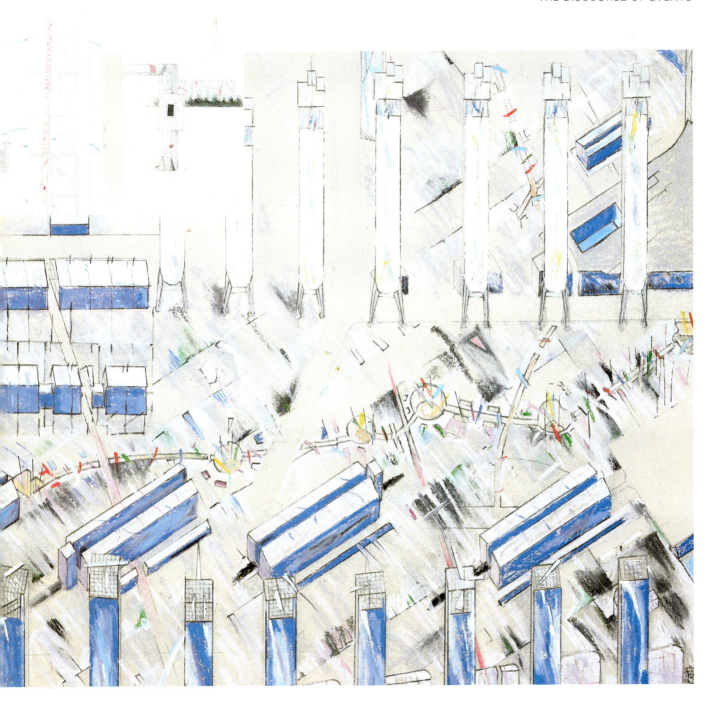

The EoA '81

Ken Yoshimura

My intention here was to explore the visual relationship between the opposing groups that make up the Exhibition of Architecture's 5,000 inhabitants. Perhaps the differences, the tensions between people could give a cutting edge to high density life-styles. So this exhibition depends on pitching types of housing at one another.

Young couples, who live in the 'show wall' housing, enjoy displaying their lifestyles. They know that they're in full view of the families living in the scooped housing below.

Nestled between these walls and terraces, old buildings have been converted into a range of amenity institutions. Between the parallel walls of singles housing, in what effectively is the core of the site, a supermarket of lifestyle options arranges its pavilions around the old church now operating as a beauty emporium. Who would have thought that 1951's essay in the spiritual qualities of expressionist brickwork would turn out to be the kind of place where you work out and shape up?

In the *Exhibition of Architecture,* people living in it will be going about their business, while the public will be privileged to witness the newest ideas and speculations for the future being acted out before them

The Exhibition of Architecture, 1981, graphite and ball point on tracing

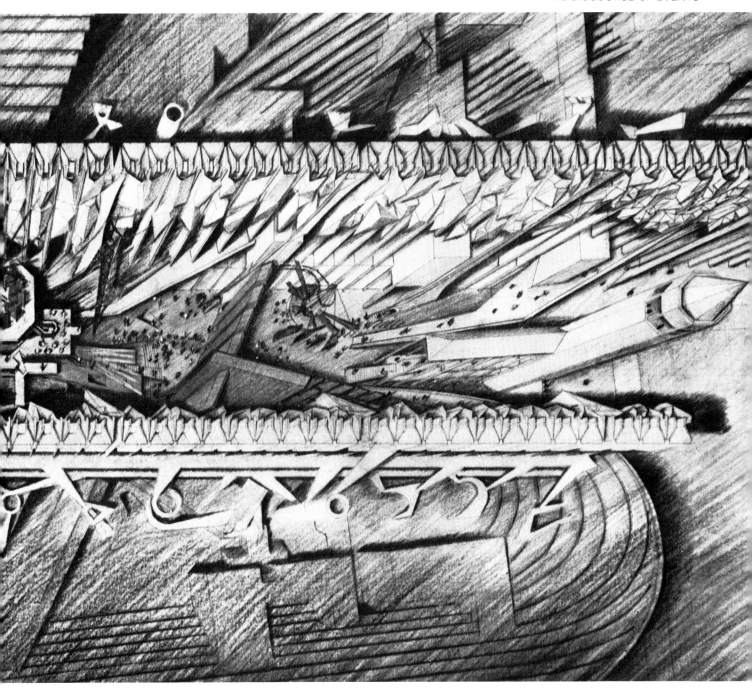

The EoA '81

Giles Prince

An interpretation: one of the more devastated areas of the London landscape, the docklands.

The hypothesis: that it is precisely the most extreme and brutal characteristics of this industrial relic that might support a London rummaging through its pockets for authenticity.

Comparisons with the torn landscape of Berlin influenced the proposals, as did Schinkel's romantic fascination with the industrial north of England. But the memory of the Festival of Britain's interest in this site (as an exhibition of ideal homes for the returning heroes of the Second World War) created the real opportunity to 'exhibit' certain architectural traits. As a modern development, it might even mimic the heroism of its predecessor.

The result: slicing the piece into two vertical strips, an Olympic, athletically blue line of apartment blocks strike a parallel to the endless, black swing of the East India Dock Road. To the right of them (facing the Isle of Dogs and its oceanic docks surrounded by patrols of disused cranes and superhuman warehouses), housing concentrates into a series of palatial sheds designed to upstage the lives of their inhabitants. To their left, mixing with the postwar graffiti of East End London, a petrified forest of apartment towers, uniformed and at attention, stand in formation as a kind of minefield barrier in advance of the East End tower blocks.

Architecture's ultimate project is to sustain the originality of experience; it does so by catching its occupants in their own disorientation

The Exhibition of Architecture, 1981, oil pastel and acrylic on canvas

Giant Sized Baby Town

that the experience of a city would coincide with the discourse of its oppositions. So *work* was brought into new contact with the *home*, as an emblematic conjunction able to provide a basis for a new urban language.

With the unit working in three teams of five, three video tapes were produced

Fish farm, chemical works, furniture factory, information bank, and the rest, add up to a city which mixes processes with public space

which, although very different, revealed three versions of how the factory (order, repetition, product, self-repression) could combine with the home (disorder, imagination, anticipation, freedom). These videos then became the 'briefs' for a more conventional architectural enterprise, to take a section through the Isle of Dogs from river to dock and then to alter it, enrich it by using the video as a model, as a *line* in parallel to that of the section. Hence fifteen sections, fifteen new modes of production, fifteen profiles of a city.

Each author, therefore, established a site

Live projects had become something of a unit feature, but rather than working with actions alone we now decided to use video as the medium. Meanwhile, the unit began to use far coarser drawing styles. In fact the entire creative activity of the unit was focusing on the 'break-up' quality of sensations. And what could be a better way of trying it out than designing a complete 'break-up' city, on the Isle of Dogs. The year began with a project for a radio station, then through a video programme based on mixing the themes of *home* and *work* and on to a mesh of interlocked factory projects that spread over the whole of the island. *Giant Sized Baby Town*, as we called it, seemed the ideal way of unmasking a spirited kind of architecture built upon the wastes of urban decay.

From the outset, the work of the year

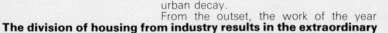

Still from *Private Works*, video

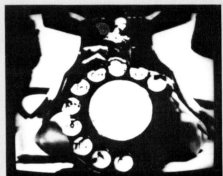

Still from *Private Works*, video

The division of housing from industry results in the extraordinary blandness familiar along every step through to Milton Keynes

hinged on the antithesis of segregation – of inducing, through architecture, a dynamic order of meaning which arises from invasions. Naturally enough, therefore, this meant pitching the old chapter headings at one another in the hope that a new vitality would emerge. Categories, divisions were not forgotten or cast out, but used to focus conflicts so

by matching the implications of the section against the surrounding topography. Most of the sites had irregular outlines, all of them reflected the basic structure of the island by occupying a 'strip' which connected the river and the dock. Settling on personal sites did, of course, involve agreement with neighbours too. Where interests coincided, because the original section lines crossed one another, it meant that certain points or landmarks on the island had to combine conflicting programmes. Four projects, for example, converged on a tiny inlet dock, three more featured the footbridge which links the east and west sides of the island.

Then more specific criteria were established. The population of the island would

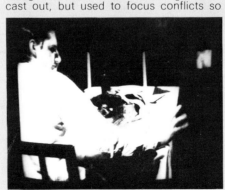

Still from *...des habitudes quotidiennes*, video

Giant Sized Baby Town's composite map

Still from Pick an' Choose, video

expand from its current 11,000 to around 40,000. In other words each author designed for 1,000 to 3,000 people, depending on the nature of the individual programme, the area and the special conditions of each site. Just how new inhabitants lived, and what they lived in, depended on the brief provided by each section line. Of course each author, with one major industrial theme of his/her own, produced a very different version of the work/home landscape. In fact they were different enough to give the kind of complementary ingredients that can be expected of a city. Fish farm, health farm, chemical works, furniture factory, infor-

usual figuration of public and private territories is lost. Looking closer, one sees that there are lines that link units of space, but not many of them seem to be roads. Conversely, the plan is a notation for pieces which must be looked at in other ways, because *Giant Sized Baby Town* has another kind of logic, one which grows out of the coercive work/home microclimate. From the start, the axis of such a proposition took form in the sequenced activities of processes; the lessons of the video and the section line had found a direct paradigm in manufacturing. In turn, the process line could replace the street as the primary space of movement and synth-

Each project's programmes held activities in deliberately suspended movement. So the buildings, for their part, played with presenting the same conundrum, fixing or solidifying whilst simultaneously unseating or detaching. You'll notice a delight in barren landscapes, old buildings isolated as monuments, or new buildings as solid towers or walls. But look again and you'll notice how every solid has been grained, or tilted. . . to permit forms and functions to invade one another.

Forget about business lunches, rush hours, or factory gates. Forget too about neat back gardens or civic flower beds; think more upon the conveyor through the kitchen, or the nightclub in an assembling hall

mation bank and the rest, added up to a city in which processes are mixed with public spaces.

In trying to gain a clear picture of the island as a whole, the plan gives precious little away. Like Piranesi's plan of the *Campo Marzio*, it beds large set-pieces into one another with such density that the

esis. Each scheme turned this principle into features which are clear enough – a path, a viaduct, a tracking crane, a system of conveyors – but their roles have changed more than you might expect, not so much in how they themselves are used, but through all the competing elements that they hold together.

The Furniture Precinct

Neil Porter

Perched on the precipice of his balcony, the householder scans the work processes below. Splicing through the scene, the track of a gantry crane links his particular view to the sequential activities which compose the territory of the furniture of the factory; an elongated form stretching right through from the river to the dock.

In fact the process begins as the crane picks up raw materials from a vast hypermarket, to carry it northwards towards the Processing Square; the place that combines public meeting with momentary glimpses of products in transit. Here materials are distributed to work halls in which a new breed of artisans live and work. They bring their materials into their living rooms – rooms which tilt inwards around the work halls, as if held by the machines. Then the various parts of furniture that emerge are passed on to an assembly plant up by Millwall Dock. This plant provides a rallying point for the whole island by doubling-up as a night-club.

Finally, the completed products are thrust out into a circular piazza to meet the watchful eyes of those inside the housing around. Here each piece is sprayed, polished and packaged, ready for dispatch as a sign of the interlocking of work and home.

GSBT is forming another kind of logic based on the work/home microclimate

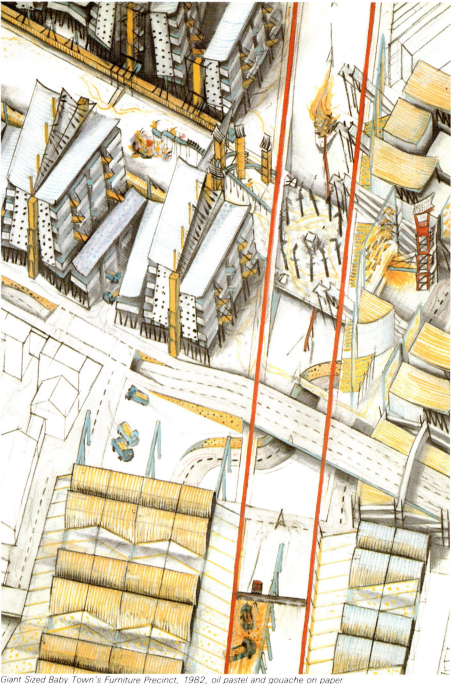

Giant Sized Baby Town's Furniture Precinct, 1982, oil pastel and gouache on paper

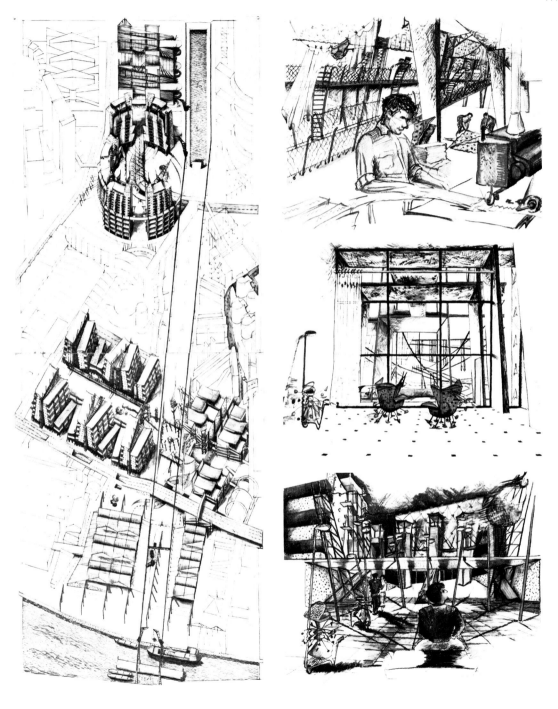

The Mannequin Project

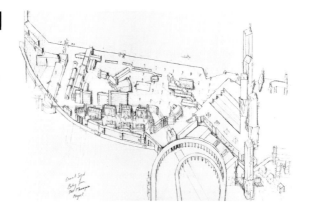

Martin Benson

Amid a landscape of mannequin sculptures, the Towers of Quality and Quantity dominate. From their vantage points on the towers, the industrialist inhabitants assess the value of the sculptures, imposing changes upon the production process – and the product itself – when they think it necessary.

Overhead display tracks, which carry the mannequins, link the various parts of the manufacturing process. Each has an effect upon the local terrain, modifying the scope of public activities and the nature of the habitation. To gain a complete picture of the process as a whole, it has to be viewed either from one of the towers or from the single direction, elevated roadway which crosses the parts of the process.

Each area has developed individual features; for example, the fabrication zone is dominated by heavy industrial buildings with a vast quantity of air-conditioning plant and the occasional smell of acrid fumes. Here life is lived at a brutal pace; many of the values are radically different from those found elsewhere. This undercurrent of difference and conflict is frequently expressed in the use of the mannequins themselves, which are altered in scale, finish, function and number in the different areas, so that not only do they become as important as the live inhabitants, but even become parts of buildings themselves.

Planning ignores the synthesising instinct, but the clashing of events can match the Paisley screen inside the mind

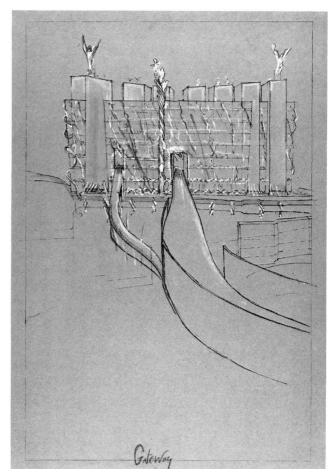

Giant Sized Baby Town's Mannequin Project, 1982, french chalk and pièrre noire on sugar paper/tracing

On-Floor Workshop

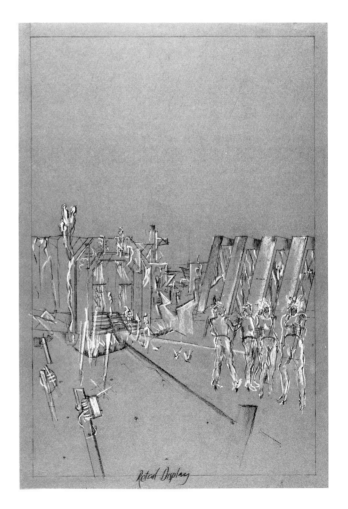

Retail Display

The Fabric Factory

Christina Norton

Lying in bed, the view through your living room to the podium beyond is eclipsed by fabric, as it slices past your window on its way to be printed. Figures can be seen winding round the bases of the three towers which mask the entrance to the fabric factory and the supermarket below. There, trucks are unloading raw materials and food.

In the other direction, you can hear the clatter of the canteen mixed with the thudding pulse of the nightclub and the fervent shrieks of bargain hunters in the supermarket – all sounds measured against the background throb of machines.

After all, new combinations of living, eating, working and dancing do spark off new lifestyles. As processes become more automated, the ritual-like events of everyday life – the freedom to 'pick-and-choose' could assume the role of work. Further on, the podium opens, exposing the vast hall of the nightclub. It has walls thick enough to contain rooms, from which pattern designers can stock up for next year's fashions by spying on the dancefloor. The room compares disco and work, anticipating their fusion. Housing and factory finally complete the cloth/clothing narrative in a huge launderette - the machine hall and gossip lounge of the future. Here the domestic action of washing one's clothes assumes city dimensions.

Sometimes brash, sometimes anxious, architecture works as a catalyst of lifestyle rather than a consolidation of stability or power

Giant Sized Baby Town's Fabric Factory, 1982, airbrush and ink on laminated paper/charcoal on paper

The Timber Fibre Factory

Carlos Villanueva

A tired crane returns to rest among the moving elements of the city.
Structures explode. An existing tower is physically dismantled, only its skeletal frame remaining. Its walls, carrying within them the life they protect, are moved to a new location. This transformation is produced by real and conceptual changes formed by a series of movements within a defined time scale. Observations of the Isle of Dogs and video images combine with a framework formed from industrial and intellectual processes to create an architectural language for use as a source of inspiration rather than an established set of rules.
The crane rises early and moves off to work. It arrives, establishes itself, confronts, then returns home to rest.
In the attempt to create a new city, the influences produced by the personification of the travelling crane are as important as those derived from the patterns of manufacture in the timber factory.
The tower (crane) swings past the tower (dog), which welcomes its tired friend.
The fragment of the Isle of Dogs forming the site can be divided into four sections. The *tower*, inhabited by stacks of drying timber, stands upright at the entrance to this part of the island. Heating, burning and stacking, mingled with the fumes and sulphur, create a centre of activity. Transparent *wall-houses* face the tower and join the fabric and motorbike factories in the chaos of the lorry park. *Venice*, a tightly designed structure, similar to a multi-storey car park, encourages active dialogue between different life styles. The *shed*, which protects the finished timber products, houses an enormous fireplace and canteen and is a stable fixture in the city. From it activity radiates, as the timber panels shift from the shed to innumerable destinations. The industrial piazza sets up a dialogue between the two factory lines, referring both to the dock and the street.
The crane stirs at rest.

Old buildings can be emptied and then filled up with new uses; the old function is bound to emerge under some other disguise.

Giant Sized Baby Town's Timber Fibre Factory, 1982, oil pastel, acrylic and pencil on paper

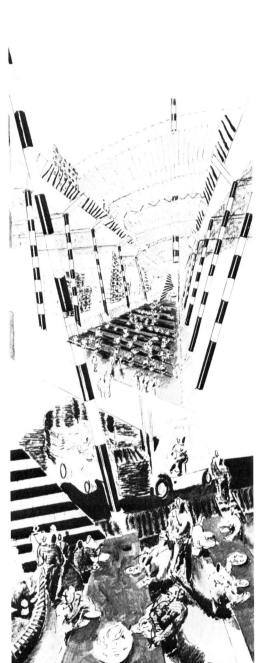

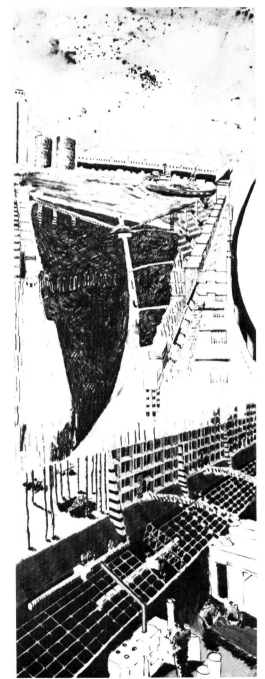

The Chemical Works

Mark Prizeman

What would life be without the *Jungle*
the animal power of the smoke stack?
An umbilical cord pumps liquid sulphur
to the heavy chemical works, by the still
dock side, from the heaving dispatch
jetty. Weaving its way across the dogs'
isle, subsidiary industries cluster, houses
breed and work is forgotten. Between
the conurbations, where the pylons
stride, lie the saharas of wilderness
punctuated by the odd cafe or pink
rubber cone. Taking a walk across these
wastes one views the hives of activity as
a warren for the creative senses. For
work here is not treated as a means to
an endless supply of Cortinas and Sandy
Shaw records but as a trigger to enable
minds to fester.

Transversing the pharmaceutical factory
is a large canteen. Industrial cooking
facilities are provided, prams pass dinner
parties, the factory hooter sounds,
donating a note to a moment in time to
start work or go to bed. The workers by
the magazine stall, trying to stay awake
on dawn aides, pick their noses and
gaze at the aircraft dismantling yard
across the road. Lorries swoosh past in
the drizzle, the argon cutter faintly
illuminates the storage tanks casting long
shadows on the depot hotels, someone
changes a record over and a few notes
change hands.

Lying on your back, the sodium orange
lights rest in stripes across the persian
carpet. Looking out of the window, the
waste pipes burst like an exhaust driving
you towards the intoxication of distant
highly illuminated towers, chimneys and
ramps.

**REV-REV a smart car, furrry dice, a trip to sandy shores
with a punch card operator, a few jars and a protex blue?**

Giant Sized Baby Town's Chemical Works, 1982, charcoal on paper/acrylic, and pencil on tracing

Bernard Tschumi
Born 1944, French-Swiss. Studied in Paris and Zurich (E.T.H. Dipl. Architect, Federal Institute of Technology). Lives in New York City. Taught at the AA from 1970, starting unit illustrated in this catalogue in 1973. Taught at the Institute for Architecture and Urban Studies in New York 1976 and Princeton University 1980-82. Currently Visiting Professor at Cooper Union School of Architecture in New York. Has published widely, including a book of theoretical projects entitled The Manhattan Transcripts. *Major exhibitions of his drawings have been held in the United States and Europe, including the Centre Pompidou in Paris and the Max Protetch Gallery in New York. His theoretical constructions, 'The 20th Century Follies', have been built in New York, London and Holland. Was recently awarded Joint First Prize in* La Villette *International Competition in Paris.*

Nigel Coates
Born 1949, British. Studied at Nottingham University and the AA, graduating with a year prize in 1974. Awarded Italian Government scholarship to Rome University in 1978. Has taught at the AA 1974-75, and 1977 to date, becoming Unit Master in 1979, and at Bennington College, Vermont, 1980-81. Has published extensively, including AD, Harper's & Queen *and* AA Files. *Has exhibited in London, Italy and the US. Work has ranged from collaboration in the performing arts, such as set design and the drawings for the film* The Draughtsman's Contract *through to large installations and the more recent 'painted drawings'.*

John Andrews
Born 1950, British. Studied at Chelsea School of Art and at the AA, graduating with a year prize 1975. Worked in New York and Mexico City, Unit Master at AA since 1980, and teaching at Cambridge.
Ron Arad
Born 1951, Israeli. Studied at Jerusalem Academy of Art and design and at the AA, graduating 1980. Opened One-Off the furniture workshop and showroom in 1981.
Jeremy Barnes
Born 1954, British. Studied at Canterbury College of Art and at the AA, graduating with honours, 1980. Since running own practice in Jersey.

Joao Basto
Born 1951, Portuguese. Studied at Lisbon University of Fine Art and at the AA, graduating 1975. Since working in London, Belgium and Macau. Has exhibited installations in Hong Kong and Lisbon.
Martin Benson
Born 1957, British. Studied at the AA, graduating 1982. Since working on a Mayfair shop project with Nigel Coates.

Doug Branson
Born 1957, British. Studied at Canterbury College of Art and at the AA, graduating 1975. Currently running own small practice in London.

James Campbell
Born 1955, Canadian. Studied at the University of Waterloo and at the AA, graduating 1982. Currently working in private practice in London.

Rosemary Ind
Born 1933, British. Studied at the AA, graduating 1974. Open University Course Tutor for the history of architecture and design. Currently preparing a book on John Emberton to be published in spring 1983.
Murray John
Born 1952, British. Studied at the London College of Furniture, and at the AA, graduating 1981. Currently running own designer/builder office in London.
Lisette Khalastchi
Born 1957, British. Studied at Manchester University and at the AA, graduating 1982. Worked in Paris 1980-81. Currently working with Foster Associates.
Jenny Lowe
Born 1951, Australian. Studied at Melbourne University and at the AA, graduating with a year prize 1974. Teaching with Bernard Tschumi 1974-5 and Intermediate Tutor 1978 to date (Unit Mistress 1980). Work shown in London, USA and the Venice Biennale in 1980.
Chris Macdonald
Born 1953, Canadian. Studied at the AA, graduating with honours 1979. AA Unit Master 1980-82. Now concentrating on enlarging the extent and scope of private work.
Christina Norton
Born 1959, British. Studied at the Bartlett School of Architecture, University of London and at the AA. Currently a member of Diploma Unit 10.

Socrates Panayides
Born 1954, Greek Cypriot. Studied at the Polytechnic of Central London and at the AA, graduating in 1981. Working in own practice in Cyprus since 1981. General Secretary of the Cyprus Architects' Association.
John Perver
Born 1951, British. Studied at the AA, graduating in 1979. Set up own office in 1979. Short period of teaching at the AA in 1981.

Neil Porter
Born 1958, British. Studied at Newcastle University School of Architecture and at the AA. Currently a member of Diploma Unit 1.

Giles Prince
Born 1957, British. Studied at Manchester University School of Architecture and at the AA. Currently a member of Diploma Unit 6. Set up own design consultancy in 1981. Has worked in offices in London and Rome.
Mark Prizeman
Born 1959, British. Studying at the AA. Currently a member of Diploma Unit 10.

Derek Revington
Born 1950, Canadian. Studied at the AA, graduating with a year prize 1975. Currently working with A.J. Diamond & Associates. Graduate student mentor at the University of British Columbia.
John Ryba
Born 1953, Australian. Studied interior design at the Hornsey College of Art and at the AA, graduating in 1979. Currently working in Australia.

Anthony Summers
Born 1951, Canadian. Studied at the Memorial University of Newfoundland, the University of Manitoba and the AA, graduating with honours, 1979. Currently teaching at the AA with Intermediate Unit 5.
Duane Van Dyke
Born 1959, American. Studied at the University of Miami and for a short period at the AA in 1980, graduating 1981. Currently working in Cleveland, Ohio.
Carlos Villanueva
Born 1954, Venezuelan. Studied at the AA, graduating 1982. Currently in practice in London.

Karen Wainer
Born 1954, Israeli. Studied at Tel Aviv University and at the AA, graduating 1981. Has worked with Mike Gold and Bernard Tschumi on competitions. Has worked in many offices, most recently with John Melvin & Partners.
Ken Yoshimura
Born 1948, Japanese. Studied at Waseda University and at the AA, graduating 1981. Currently working at Lasdun, Redhouse & Softley.

Acknowledgements

In particular we would like to thank Alvin Boyarsky for his steadfast support, mixed with just enough provocation to stimulate progress, Peter Cook for continual encouragement, Jenny Lowe for her shared concerns, and Martin Benson, without whom this catalogue simply would not exist.

We owe many thanks to Gianni Pettena, Leon van Shaik, Ricardo Pais and Tony Carruthers, all of whom have run special short projects with great success, and our technical tutors John Lyall, Richard Padovan, and Andrew Walker.

We would also like to thank all those architects, fellow teachers, artists, critics and friends who have made invaluable contributions to the unit in the form of lectures, juries, and special events. . .
RoseLee Goldberg, Brian Muller, Victor Burgin, John Stezaker, Carol McNicoll, John Hilliard, David Dye, Chris Bailey, Su Braden, Rosemary Ind, Paolo Deganello, Pietro Derossi, Antoine Grumbach, Christian de Portzamparc, Rene Tabouret, Fernando Mantes, Elaine Potter, Ron Hall, Thanos Skouras, Peppino Ortoleva, Germano Celant, Will Alsop, Fred Scott, Rem Koolhaas, Elia Zenghelis, Bob Evans, Bob Maxwell, Peter Wilson, Rosetta Brooks, Bruce McLean, COUM, Genesis P'orridge, Brian Eno, Clive Tempest, David Greene, Peter Wilson, Crispin Osborne, Billy Walton, Peter York, Barbara Brownfield, Zaha Hadid, Ferry Zayadi, Doug Branson, Martin Chapman, Raimund Abraham, Willie Jefferies, Gordon Benson, António Lagarto, John Perver, Rochelle Feinstein, Nigel Tuersley, Don Gray, Barbara Tyrell, Derek Jarman, Salina Fellows, Patrick Kinmonth and John Outram.

Lastly, but perhaps most importantly, it remains to thank all who have worked in the unit for their diligent studentship, especially those participating in this current show, the *Discourse of Events*. . .